Comments on other *Amazing Stories* from readers & reviewers

"Tightly written volumes filled with lots of wit and humour about famous and infamous Canadians."
Eric Shackleton, *The Globe and Mail*

"The heightened sense of drama and intrigue, combined with a good dose of human interest is what sets Amazing Stories *apart."*
Pamela Klaffke, *Calgary Herald*

"This is popular history as it should be... For this price, buy two and give one to a friend."
Terry Cook, a reader from Ottawa, on **Rebel Women**

"Glasner creates the moment of the explosion itself in graphic detail...she builds detail upon gruesome detail to create a convincingly authentic picture."
Peggy McKinnon, *The Sunday Herald*, on **The Halifax Explosion**

"It was wonderful...I found I could not put it down. I was sorry when it was completed."
Dorothy F. from Manitoba on **Marie-Anne Lagimodière**

"Stories are rich in description, and bristle with a clever, stylish realness."
Mark Weber, *Central Alberta Advisor*, on **Ghost Town Stories II**

"A compelling read. Bertin...has selected only the most intriguing tales, which she narrates with a wealth of detail."
Joyce Glasner, *New Brunswick Reader*, on **Strange Events**

"The resulting book is one readers will want to share with all the women in their lives."
Lynn Martel, *Rocky Mountain Outlook*, on **Women Explorers**

ROBERTA BONDAR

ROBERTA BONDAR

The Exceptional Achievements of
Canada's First Woman Astronaut

BIOGRAPHY

by Joan Dixon

PUBLISHED BY ALTITUDE PUBLISHING CANADA LTD.
1500 Railway Avenue, Canmore, Alberta T1W 1P6
www.altitudepublishing.com
1-800-957-6888

Extreme care has been taken to ensure that all information presented in
this book is accurate and up to date. Neither the author nor the
publisher can be held responsible for any errors.

Publisher	Stephen Hutchings
Associate Publisher	Kara Turner
Series Editor	Jill Foran
Editor	Lori Burwash

We acknowledge the financial support of the Government
of Canada through the Book Publishing Industry Development
Program (BPIDP) for our publishing activities.

Altitude GreenTree Program
Altitude Publishing will plant twice as many trees as were used
in the manufacturing of this product.

We acknowledge the support of the Canada Council for the Arts which
in 2003 invested $21.7 million in writing and publishing throughout Canada.

Canada Council   Conseil des Arts
for the Arts   du Canada

National Library of Canada Cataloguing in Publication Data

Dixon, Joan, 1957-
  Roberta Bondar / Joan Dixon.

(Amazing stories)
Includes bibliographical references.
ISBN 1-55153-799-0

1. Bondar, Roberta Lynn, 1945-. 2. Women astronauts--Canada--
Biography. 3. Discovery (Spacecraft) I. Title. II. Series: Amazing stories
(Canmore, Alta.)

TL789.85.B66D59 2004   629.45'0092   C2004-902320-9

An application for the trademark for Amazing Stories™
has been made and the registered trademark is pending.

Printed and bound in Canada by Friesens
2 4 6 8 9 7 5 3 1

To astronauts, our surrogates in space

Contents

Prologue 11

Chapter 1 Starstruck Child 13

Chapter 2 Stepping Stones to Space 20

Chapter 3 The Biggest Competition of Her Life 30

Chapter 4 The First to Fly 42

Chapter 5 Disaster! 53

Chapter 6 Astronauts in Training 61

Chapter 7 Liftoft! 74

Chapter 8 Working on the Edge 86

Chapter 9 Living on the Edge 95

Chapter 10 Coming Down 101

Epilogue: Life on Earth 108

Appendix 1: Crew of STS-42 111

Appendix 2: Timeline 113

Appendix 3: Canada's Select Six 120

Bibliography 123

Prologue

Roberta Bondar couldn't eat. It wasn't as if she wasn't hungry. Busy and active, she was always hungry. But on this day, Saturday, December 3, 1983, she found food — even a tall, cool glass of her favourite skim milk — unappetizing. A birthday cake was sitting in her kitchen untouched. The family and friends who had gathered to help celebrate her 38th birthday a day early would have to eat it.

Roberta was waiting for a phone call — one that could change her life and fulfil a childhood dream. She and the other 18 finalists for the job she had applied for had been told to expect news this evening. Only six would make the cut.

Roberta was no stranger to competition. As a woman growing up in the 1950s and 1960s, she was used to being told she couldn't or shouldn't be doing what she was doing. But Roberta always proved them wrong. Playing basketball, tennis, and every other sport she could fit into her schedule, she thrived on the adrenaline. The more cerebral challenges came from the four degrees she had earned by the time she was 31. In all aspects of her life, Roberta had always reached for the top and made it — at least, until now.

Would Roberta succeed this time? The job she had

applied for was no ordinary job — she wanted to be the first Canadian astronaut in space. Canada was ready to send its own astronauts on the United States' space shuttle, and Roberta was determined to be one of them.

At 6:45 p.m., the phone rang. Taking a deep breath, Roberta reached to grab it.

Chapter 1
Starstruck Child

even-year-old Roberta was busy as usual with her older sister, Barbara, creating a spaceship out of cardboard and wood. "Girls, they're here!" Roberta's mother called out after the mailman had dropped off the day's delivery. Roberta was concentrating on making cockpit controls out of wire. In their elaborate fantasy world, Roberta was crew to her sister's command of the spaceship. They had a special mission lined up. The critical last component had finally arrived. Roberta raced her sister to their mother and the much anticipated package.

It was 1953 and the world was becoming more optimistic and forward-looking after enduring yet another world war. Roberta and her sister were part of the baby boom that had followed peace and its new prosperity in North America. Building on its hard-won reputation as an aircraft manufacturer and designer during the war, Canada was using aerospace technology to further its reputation as a country with a sparkling future. Roberta was already preparing to play a large role in that future.

She and her sister had eagerly saved their gum wrappers and sent away to the Double Bubble company for its special offer of space helmets. Waiting for what seemed like an eternity, young Roberta had assumed the helmets would arrive in a large box, complete with air hoses and glass covers. But all she could see in her mother's hands were two flat brown envelopes. "That can't be them," the logical child informed her sister and stopped running. When they opened the envelopes, they found two tall white rectangular pieces of cardboard, each with a large square opening in the front.

Roberta's face told the story — she was not impressed. If the older Barbara was also disappointed, she didn't show it. Unfolding hers, she said to her sister, "Let's put them on and go exploring." Off into their Sault Ste. Marie neighbourhood the sisters went, down McGregor Avenue and Edward's Lane, and on to Upton Road. They brought along their red and green Flash Gordon water pistols in case they ran into unfriendly aliens.

Family Foundations

When they weren't out on adventures, the Bondar girls enveloped themselves in a world of fact and fiction. As a young girl, Roberta spent much of her spare time dreaming about rockets and planets, and most of her favourite activities had something to do with space. While her sister chose to build plastic models of ships and airplanes, Roberta preferred models of rockets, space stations, and satellites that hadn't yet been invented. They usually spent Saturday mornings enthralled with the radio adventures of Tom Corbett on a fictitious alien space station in *Space Cadet*. One of the characters, Dr. Joan Dale — a professor and research pioneer who invented hyperdrive — was a woman out of her time. She could have served as an alternative role model for the ambitious Bondar girls, whose adventurous mother encouraged their dreams.

Roberta read every book in the library about space, including the sci-fi Classic Comics versions of *From the Earth to the Moon*. Images of solar eclipses thanks to the foresighted Jules Verne helped to colour her imagination. Reading a precursor to *Star Trek* called *Assignment in Space*, she pictured herself as none other than the intrepid explorer Rip Foster.

Despite the fact no one had yet made it into space, except in the science fiction novels she read, young Roberta was determined to make it her own destiny. To be a star voyager was the most exciting thing she could imagine: she foresaw "brave new worlds, adventure, living on the edge, using my knowledge, and my skills, being a pioneer and an explorer."

Roberta was certainly never brought down to Earth by her parents. Edward and Mildred Bondar wanted more for their daughters than what they had managed for themselves. Edward's own parents were Russian emigrants who settled in Sault Ste. Marie, Ontario, in the early 1900s for a more hopeful future. And although he was called "Know-It-All Eddie" in high school, the bright and hardworking Edward couldn't afford to go to university in the times of war and the Great Depression. Instead, he served in the 49th Field Artillery and worked as a manager of the local utilities commission.

Edward met Mildred in high school. She had been their class valedictorian, but was also unable to attend university at the time. (She would earn a degree later, at 48, and eventually teach business.) Mildred and Edward married after World War II. They focused their energies on their young daughters, wanting to help them be the best they could be.

Roberta's parents believed that one can learn as much outside of school as inside it. As a result, young Roberta was busy with a variety of after-school activities, such as Brownies, church groups, sports at the YMCA — anything that might ensure a well-rounded childhood. "They never [just] dropped us off," Barbara remembered of their parents. They were there to cheer their girls on. Edward spent hours in their backyard building a skating rink for his girls and the neighbourhood kids. In their basement, he built a lab so that Roberta could conduct experiments with the microscope their pharmacist uncle had given them. For her birthdays, Roberta asked for a chemistry set, a model rocket kit, and a doctor's bag. The sports equipment she hoped for usually came later the same month, at Christmastime.

The Bondars encouraged all sports and outdoor activities. Barbara recalled they were never subjected to stereotypes. "We jumped out of trees and played with dolls." Edward taught the technically minded Roberta how to handle both tools and guns, unusual skills for girls at that time.

Photography was another interest Edward shared with his daughters. Both he and the girls' Uncle Arthur delighted in taking 35 mm photos and 8 mm movies of family adventures on the lake. Roberta was thrilled when she received her own camera one year — a Brownie camera with black and white film. Used to the colour slides in her 3-D View-Master, she was initially disappointed with the restrictions of black and white. Soon, however, she was hooked. With her parents encouraging her to record the world around, photography became an integral part of her experiences.

When Roberta wasn't playing intrepid explorer in space, she was still exploring, but in the great Northern Ontario outdoors. Weekend trips to the nearby shores of Lake Superior with her family taught her to appreciate nature by examining it closely. (But she wasn't convinced all nature was worth appreciating — she was initially uncomfortable with bugs.)

The youngest Bondar always insisted on packing as much of her space equipment as she could into the car. Sitting by the fire at night, she would watch the sparks, imagining them travelling up into the stars that she was convinced beckoned to her. She wanted to see what her Earth and other planets looked like. "I longed to soar into space, reaching out to adventure with my body as well as my imagination."

Space Race

Roberta was not alone in her desire to reach space. The plastic models she was building by the time she was 11 were miniature replicas of the early American *Vanguard* satellites. The Soviet Union had just beaten the U.S. in launching the first satellite, *Sputnik,* into space in 1957. (Unfortunately, it was on the same day Canada's new supersonic jet fighter, the Avro Arrow, was unveiled. Canada's triumph was eclipsed.) The race for space had officially begun and Roberta was paying close attention. Her fantasies were becoming real, spurred on by the international politics of the Cold War.

In 1959, when Roberta was 13, she was proud to hear of the aerospace efforts of her own country. The first flight of Canada's *Black Brant* rocket pioneered scientific research into microgravity. The next year, the U.S. launched the world's first communications satellite, *Echo 1.* Roberta raced along the shore of Lake Superior to watch it streak across the night sky.

Like her immediate family, Roberta's extended family

was convinced she would go far. By this time, her Aunt Erma was living and working in Florida, along with many Canadian aerospace engineers who migrated to NASA after the Arrow project was cancelled. She regularly sent the eager Roberta news of the burgeoning U.S. space program and posters that her niece wasted no time plastering on her bedroom wall.

Roberta, like her country, was curious to find out what was beyond Earth's boundaries. With such a dynamic and supportive family life nurturing her curiosity, it was no wonder this cheerful, bright adolescent was convinced she could do anything and was determined to do just that. From early on, she had decided life was going to be an adventure, on Earth and, with any luck, in space.

Chapter 2
Stepping Stones
to Space ...

 eaving grade school behind, Roberta moved on to the local high school, Sir James Dunn Collegiate and Vocational School. It was not yet the Age of Aquarius, when young people found individualism fashionable and rejected the mainstream, but Roberta was never one to follow a crowd anyway — and she didn't let stereotyping bully her from her ambitions. She remembers her high school years as being character building: "You don't realize how formative they are at the time."

When Roberta was in grade 13, the guidance counsellor tried to discourage her from taking science, telling her mom she didn't work hard enough. At the time, boys were supposed to choose science for their future work, while girls were encouraged to study the arts. Mildred responded, "Roberta will do whatever she wants to do." Roberta's focus continued to be the sciences. She produced a memorable project on the Moon. She led the science club. To overcome her dislike of insects, she studied the life cycle of tent caterpillars for a science experiment. The project won second prize at the City Science Fair and honourable mention at the Canada Wide Science Fair and eventually led to summer research jobs. In the culture of the time, when girls were discouraged from pursuing the same educational goals as boys, Roberta thought, "Nonsense! I'm as capable as a male!" She might have inherited this feisty temperament from her mother, whose favourite saying was "To thine own self be true."

What also set Roberta apart was her affinity for sports — also considered more the domain of men at the time. Roberta preferred activity. She wanted to play all the sports and join all the clubs — her green cardigan was plastered with participation badges. Basketball was her favourite team sport, but she played them all. She arranged camping and canoe trips and found kindred spirits with whom to hike and fish. On canoe trips, she would imagine she was the intrepid voyageur. As she put it, she was never good at "sitting around chewing the fat." In her second last year of high school, Roberta was selected Female Athlete of the Year.

But it wasn't as easy or automatic as it appeared. In grade nine, in fact, Roberta did not make the junior basketball team. "I was devastated when the coach didn't choose me." But she was not about to give up. Coached by Barbara, she practised every day for a year. The next year, her determination paid off when she made the senior team. However, she still felt the sting of not earning the junior basketball badge. Much later, at her high school graduating ceremony, Roberta was presented with an honorary grade 9 basketball crest — to her great surprise and thrill. Her incredible badge collection was now complete.

During these busy high school years, the space race was heating up. On April 12, 1961, the Soviet cosmonaut Yuri Gagarin became the first person to successfully fly in space. On May 25, 1961, United States President John F. Kennedy made his famous promise — the Apollo program would put a man on the Moon by the end of that decade. Later, he told students, "We choose to go to the Moon in this decade not because it is easy but because it is hard." (And of course because of the competition from their Cold War enemy, the Soviet Union.) The Apollo program was certainly one of the most technically complex projects of the 20th century, and Roberta naturally wanted to be part of it. Like many of her generation, she followed each rocket launch with fascination, imagining herself cramped in the capsules alongside the astronauts.

In 1962, Canada joined the space race with *Alouette*, becoming the third nation in the world to put a satellite in orbit. This began Canada's long collaboration with the U.S. in space. Although the Canadian aerospace industry was burgeoning, Roberta couldn't help but notice that the field was still predominantly the domain of men.

Before finishing high school, Roberta needed to make some decisions about the future. What did she want to be? Although she dreamed of space, science, and medicine, she more pragmatically set her sights on becoming a teacher — the highest career ambition for many students at that time. In the meantime, she was going to learn everything she could about all the things that interested her and see where that took her.

Undergrad Epiphany

During her high school years, Roberta spent her summers working at the local "bug lab" run by the Department of Fisheries and Forestry (referred to as the Department of Fish and Chips). It was a good thing she had overcome her discomfort with bugs — she had to study the spruce bud worm, which feeds off Canadian trees and causes great damage to the environment. This hands-on research would prove to be a significant experience in the budding naturalist's and environmentalist's career path. It helped her see the potential for a career as a scientist.

The scientists at the department convinced Roberta to study biology at the University of Guelph in southern Ontario. The small, friendly campus was rural in location and nature, not intimidating like the city universities. There, Roberta could continue to play sports and pursue all sorts of other interests, including the study of zoology and agriculture, for which Guelph was renowned.

When Roberta began her undergraduate studies in 1964, she couldn't have guessed that she would eventually spend 18 years on various campuses earning four academic degrees. Of course the academic work at Guelph didn't keep her nearly busy or interested enough at first. She played basketball and played on and coached the archery team. With her first 35 mm camera, she also played photojournalist, capturing university life on colour slides. She had a quick smile and a lively sense of humour and made friends easily. One of her professors, Dr. Roy Anderson, described her as "a real all-rounder" and "outgoing, warm, direct." The turning point in Roberta's academic career came in third year, when her scholarly side finally emerged. Confined to bed with a bad case of the mumps for what seemed an interminably long time, all Roberta could do was study. Her grades soared as a result.

By 1968, not only had Roberta received her Bachelor of Science degree, she had added an equally important building block in her career plans — a private pilot's licence. She had learned to fly single-engine planes during summer holidays, too.

Pilots-turned-astronauts had been blasting off into space on an almost regular basis in the Gemini and Apollo programs all through Roberta's undergraduate years. The last few years of the decade had been particularly exciting, especially for astronaut wannabes like Roberta. Men had finally landed on the Moon in the lunar lander *Eagle* — only a few nail-biting months before Kennedy's deadline. On July 20, 1969, Roberta ran back and forth from her parents' porch, where she could see the Moon itself, to the TV, where she could see Neil Armstrong and Buzz Aldrin actually walking on the Moon.

Master's Work

The moonstruck 23-year-old Roberta still didn't know what to do next. Her professors at Guelph recognized that she was graduate school material, but that she also hadn't hit her potential. Roberta understood she needed outstanding grades to go into medicine, but she hadn't earned the necessary marks. It simply hadn't been a goal.

Roberta applied to graduate school at the University of Western Ontario in London with scholarships and savings from her summer job. When accepted, she requested to do research on the heart in the department of pathology. There, she encountered a stern taskmaster in Dr. Daria Haust, an important mentor who would not stand for anything less than perfection. Roberta soon confirmed she had the ability to focus complete attention on a subject until she had acquired all the knowledge available.

By 1971, the end of her Master's degree in experimental pathology, Roberta had completed a research project on the effect of high blood pressure on rats' hearts that was quoted for decades afterward. She had worked part-time as a teaching assistant but enjoyed the research most. She had also begun to record and support her science work with another of her continuing passions, photography, developing new techniques for colour photo-microscopy.

Double Doctor

Roberta's interests in space and photography intersected in 1972, when she marvelled at the unimpeded views of the marblelike Earth from the final Apollo mission. The space shuttle program had recently been announced, along with a new law supposed to end NASA's discrimination of women in its astronaut recruitment. Soon Canada's *Anik* communications satellite, as well as the Soviet Union's space station, would clutter the view of — and from — space. Space did not seem so far away anymore.

Although she would have preferred to be taking her own pictures of space, 26-year-old Roberta was still in school. She was now doing her PhD at the University of Toronto, studying the fish's central nervous system and how the brains of goldfish were affected by the water temperature. This was an experimental model for changes seen in the brains of humans with Alzheimer's disease. She completed her doctorate in neurobiology, all the while working extensively with black and white photography.

By now, Roberta was considered a well organized, calm,

and professional researcher. Her professors were not sur-prised when, in 1974, she applied to medical school so that she could be an even more qualified clinical researcher. She thought being a doctor would also better equip her to help humanity — besides, she finally had the marks to get in.

In 1977, at the age of 31, Roberta graduated with a med-ical degree from McMaster University, with a special interest in space medicine. After completing her board certification in neurology, she studied at Tufts-New England Medical Center in Boston, specializing in neurophthalmology, the science of how we see and record the world around us. As a doctor, Roberta was gentle, careful, and kind with patients. But as one of her professors, Dr. Andrew Talalla, astutely recognized, "This wasn't going to be an ordinary doctor who disappeared into private practice."

After 18 years of study and research, Roberta had achieved two career goals: scientist and medical doctor. But as she completed more years of post-graduate medical train-ing in London, Toronto, and Boston, she was still unsure of where she would go and what she would do next. Then, while in Boston in 1981, she watched, fascinated, the orbital flight of the first space shuttle, *Columbia.* The test flight with only two pilot-astronauts on board proved that the shuttle could reach orbit and return to land safely. Roberta had not forgot-ten this other goal. She, like NASA, had even more ambitious plans for the future.

Life After School

Despite her intense commitment to her studies, Roberta had had a busy and rich extra-curricular life pursuing her many interests. She still loved to play sports, go on camping trips, and target shoot. She made lots of friends, who appreciated her energy, dedication to fun, and good conversation. And any chance she had, she would return to her hometown and the white clapboard two-storey family home.

Like her sister, Barbara, Roberta was still unmarried, which was perhaps not unusual for professional women, but it was for 30-something women at that time. In her sister's opinion, this was because "after seeing our parents' marriage, neither of us [was] prepared to settle for anything less." But the more direct Roberta always laughed and reminded those who asked, "I've had no time for marriage — what do you think I am, for heaven's sake? Superwoman?"

In 1982, 36-year-old Roberta was invited to return to McMaster University to fulfil her high school goal of becoming a teacher. It was a big move — she was named an assistant professor of medicine in neurology and became the director of the multiple sclerosis clinic. Happy in clinical work, research, and writing articles for journals, she built on her reputation in science. Roberta concentrated on the body's nervous system — especially as it related to the functioning of the eye. She also considered doing yet more training in a complementary field — aviation medicine.

Still flying, Roberta was active with the Flying Physicians

Association, the Ninety-Nines International Organization of Women Pilots, and the Canadian Society of Aviation Medicine. And although she was pursuing her dreams of working as a teacher, a doctor, and a scientist, she still wanted to fly in space, even if not as a pilot. By this time, NASA's shuttle flights included a new category of astronaut, mission specialists, responsible only for the mission's specialized objective. This raised the hopes of astronaut wannabes everywhere, including Roberta. "I never watched a NASA launch without wanting to be on board," she reflected. But, with her living in Canada, it still seemed like an outrageous dream.

Chapter 3
The Biggest Competition of Her Life

ll of a sudden, being Canadian became an advantage. One midsummer day in 1983, Roberta was driving to her job at McMaster, tuned in to the CBC for the one o'clock time check. Instead, she heard something she had been waiting to hear all her life. The announcer was commenting on the unusual help wanted ad that the National Research Council (NRC) had put in the paper: "Seeking Canadian men and women to fly as astronauts on future space shuttle missions."

The announcer went on to list the NRC's main requirements. Roberta checked them off mentally, one by one. Adventurous spirit? No hesitation here, this had been her modus operandi since she was a little girl. Degrees and experience in engineering or in life sciences? Not only was Roberta now a medical doctor, she held several degrees, including a doctorate in neurobiology. The ad even mentioned the field of vestibular physiology — her specialty. Medical fitness? With no problems healthwise, she was as fit and keen on physical exercise as ever. Flying experience? Roberta had had her pilot's licence for 15 years by then. The rest of the criteria rushed by. She couldn't help but think the ad read "Roberta Bondar, where are you?" She was 37 and had been grooming herself for this job all her life.

Obstacles Overcome

Until 1978, all astronaut candidates at NASA were men, even though this had been ruled discriminatory in 1972. All of them also had to be experimental jet test pilots from the military. At the time, women were not allowed in combat or test pilot positions. Consequently, there were no female astronauts during Roberta's university years, despite there being interested and physically qualified pilots petitioning NASA. The first American woman in space — astrophysicist Sally Ride — flew in 1983, 20 years after the first woman in space, Soviet Valentina Tereshkova. The Soviet Union chose its cosmonauts differently — Valentina had been a textile worker and a talented amateur skydiver.

After 1978, the biggest obstacle to Roberta's astronaut career plan had, however, not been her gender, but her nationality. Until 1983, NASA had included only Americans in its space program. Ulf Merbold from Germany became the first non-American astronaut when he flew that year as a payload specialist, a new category of astronaut that was responsible for only the mission's specialized payload. (The payload was what paid for the trip: it could mean launching a satellite or conducting science experiments.) Merbold's success opened the door for space researchers and astronaut wannabes from other countries.

NASA had finally decided that international participation was critical to its future funding. In part due to the overwhelming success of the $100 million Canadarm, another product of Canadian aerospace technology, Canada was invited to fly on the shuttle. By September 1982, this invitation was reiterated formally during the 20th anniversary celebration of U.S.-Canada cooperation in space.

There were still restrictions on the invitation. NASA wanted all non-Americans to serve only as payload or mission specialists, not pilots. Canada decided it would provide its expertise and personnel in payload specialists (the scientists), rather than mission specialists (the technical operators). In 1983, the NRC set up the Canadian Astronaut Program and sent out the call for astronauts. Later that year, it was sifting through thousands of applications, including Roberta's.

Narrowing the List

Like all NASA astronaut candidates to date, Roberta fit the personality profile — a high achiever who was self-confident without arrogance. Throughout her intellectual, athletic, and recreational pursuits, she had demonstrated strong motivation and discipline and proven her ability to learn quickly and on the fly. On top of all that, she was clearly ambitious, extroverted, and articulate, not necessarily important qualifications for a space scientist, but very important for the public relations work she would have to do on behalf of the Canadian space program within Canada and NASA.

Even with all these sterling qualities, would Roberta make the cut? She crossed her fingers and mailed her application within 48 hours of hearing the announcement. The deadline for applications had to be extended because of the flood of enquiries. The agency handling the selection process had expected 1000 responses. It received 4300. Of the many schoolchildren, the youngest applicant was 6 years old. Accountants, fire fighters, dentists, skydivers, and teachers all applied for the job of astronaut. Eleven percent of the applicants were women. Of these, one was a 73-year-old housewife. Space fever had hit the Canadian public.

The first cuts the agency made were by paper. Any applicants who met the minimum professional and educational requirements but who weren't between 4'10" and 6'3", did not have blood pressure of 140 over 90 at maximum, and could not prove they had topnotch eyes and ears and no other disabilities wouldn't hear from the agency. The rest were given more detailed application forms to fill out.

The Final 19

Soon the 1606 initially qualified applicants became 68. Then, by November 1983, there were only 19 finalists: 15 English-speaking males, 3 bilingual Francophone males, and 1 woman. At each of the four stages of the process, Roberta assured her parents she probably had no chance of making it to the next round. She didn't want to worry them.

Since the general public and media seemed so interested, the agency announced the names of the 19 short-listed. Roberta remembers the surprise of this publicity. She was deluged by requests for interviews — even at her medical clinics. She suddenly found herself more popular as a doctor and began seeing quite a few people whom she called "conspicuously healthy." One of them gave her a ceramic seagull with one wingtip pointing up and "Good Luck" written on the base.

The 19 finalists were invited to a further screening process together in Ottawa late in November 1983. All well-rounded extroverts, they remember bonding as campers do in camp. Roberta's razor-sharp mind, combined with her relaxed manner, won her a lot of friends. Even though they were competing for only six spots, the finalists developed strong camaraderie between sessions at the hotel and test facilities. They even collected one another's autographs.

One night, a group of them went to a movie, the newly released *The Right Stuff,* about the Mercury astronauts in the early 1960s. The publicity for the movie made the Canadian contenders for space even hotter news. After all, it was Canada's chance to experience the hoopla of space, not just as observers this time. The astronaut candidates had to good-naturedly endure the resulting jokes about having "the right stuff" and being space cadets, even though most of them saw themselves as scientific adventurers, not heroes.

It was now up to a special committee of the National Research Council to find out who these 19 candidates were. Which of them were the most suitable to send into space, and into the limelight? The final part of the screening process was excruciatingly formal and detailed, even after six months of paperwork testing and interviewing that covered much of the same ground. The interviews were described as brutal by one of Roberta's fellow candidates, Steve MacLean. "The questions were probing, but worse than that, the interviewers were stonefaced interrogators who were programmed not to react to us." Even when the candidates tried to alleviate some of the circumstance's natural stress with jokes, no one on the interview committee laughed. This was serious business. Psychological tests, security checks, physical examinations, and stringent eye tests followed one after the other as NRC officials poked and prodded the candidates.

After being stabbed with needles at least 21 times, the sole woman was expected to face yet one more test, a pregnancy test. But because she put her social insurance number — not her name — on the urine sample, the urine samples of the 18 men also had to be tested. Later, she teased the testers, "How many were pregnant?"

Throughout most of the evaluation, Roberta and the other candidates didn't know what the examiners were looking for, or if the interviewers themselves even knew. Steve MacLean agreed, "You just had to be yourself and hope that was what they wanted." But he also said the group of 19 was the most impressive collection of individuals he had ever met. He was not alone in his assessment.

The press was glued to any new developments, feeding the public appetite with information on potential new heroes. One observer called the session a high-tech beauty pageant, with the criteria of education and physical fitness replacing the traditional ones of beauty and poise. The NRC saw it as another opportunity to test the potential astronauts' communication and media skills.

Finally it was all over. On the last day of November, the 19 candidates went home to wait for the results, still in the dark about what was considered "the right stuff" and if indeed they had it. They were told only to expect a call the following Saturday.

Getting the News

On December 3, NRC Personnel Chief Ray Dolan took to the telephone in Ottawa, as promised, between 6:00 and 7:00 in the evening. First he called the unsuccessful candidates to relay the disappointing news but also to encourage them for future opportunities in space. The frontier of space had recently opened for Canadians; many hoped it was just the beginning.

Then Dolan called the six successful astronauts. He started out mischievously discussing the weather, which most of them had in common, living or working close by in Ontario and Quebec. Dr. Ken Money was one of the two out of the area. He was preparing to work the night shift for NASA in Mission Control in Houston so was still contentedly asleep when the call came. He had expected the nod because of his 20 years' experience with space research and NASA. So when his wife informed him earlier that arrangements had been made for him to go to Ottawa the next day, he concluded he'd made it. (In fact, similar tentative arrangements had been made for all 19 candidates, so Ken was not the only one who celebrated prematurely.)

Doctor and engineer Robert Thirsk's reaction to the news was to share his good fortune. The BC native immediately proposed to his girlfriend. Twenty-eight-year-old laser researcher Steve MacLean, whom Roberta had nicknamed "the kid," did what only a young world-class gymnast could do easily — a back flip on the spot. Like Roberta, he had fantasized about that moment since he was a kid. Bjarni Tryggvason, originally hailing from Iceland and British Columbia, was already an NRC employee but reacted like he had won the lottery. He could now combine his scientific research with his passion for flying. Marc Garneau had to act like the naval commander he was, cool and collected, because he knew his young children would have trouble keeping a secret. He told only his wife, whom he'd had answer the phone.

And where was Roberta? She was celebrating her 38th birthday one day early with friends and family. Barbara noted they had gathered at Roberta's place in Dundas, Ontario, to "cheer Roberta if she made it, or support her if she didn't." The hype about the selection decision had been increasing for the past few days, and while she'd had no trouble sleeping, Roberta had found she couldn't eat because of the suspense.

The phone rang in the crowded, noisy apartment at 6:45. "Hi, Ray, fine … how are you? Am I what?" Roberta deafened her caller with a whoop of excitement and disbelief when Dolan repeated his question, "Are you ready to travel again?" Her eyes were wide and sparkling when she turned to her guests with a thumbs up. "I'm in. I'm in!"

Even if it made them a little apprehensive, Roberta's parents were delighted by her selection as an astronaut. Mildred surprised her daughter with a gift of her model rockets saved from childhood, always believing one day her daughter would fly in space. Later, Roberta would give her father a tie with space shuttles on it, to thank him for all his support. The news still felt unreal to Roberta; would she really get to experience space? Instead of just seeing the amazing photos coming down from space, would she now get the chance to take them herself?

Going Public

Roberta was lucky to be able to share the news with those closest to her at her party, but they all had to keep it a secret until the next day's press conference. To confuse the curious media, the astronaut-to-be was flown, not to Ottawa, but to Montreal to link up with Steve MacLean and Bob Thirsk. The three of them were then driven to Ottawa so any reporters staked out at the Ottawa airport would not scoop the official announcement.

With all the hoopla of a hockey draft, the candidates (excluding Ken, who remained in Houston) were presented as "men with the right stuff" by the Minister of Science and Technology, Donald Johnson. Among them, the group had 16 university scientific degrees, including 5 PhDs, 2 MDs, 3 pilots, and 2 Olympic class athletes. Their pride and enthusiasm were palpable — and infectious. They became Canada's new celebrities, made instantly famous by the media.

Despite being dressed like the others in a dark blazer, Roberta was not inconspicuous. Her frilly blouse and a rare application of make-up set her apart. As one of the Select Six, she had to respond to all the expected questions, plus the zinger — Was there a quota? Was she the token woman? (Marc Garneau also had to answer whether he felt like the token Francophone.) The official polite response was no, there was no quota. NRC representatives added they were relieved to find a candidate as qualified as Dr. Bondar — they were able to select a woman without forcing the system.

It shouldn't have been hard for the media or the public to understand why Roberta was chosen. The scientist/doctor/pilot had been preparing all her life for the space program, which would make good use of her eclectic skills and training. Her professional life could now combine science's cerebral rigours, the physical challenges of sport, and the risk taking of flying with her naturally adventurous spirit. She tried not to bristle at the questions about her gender and her capabilities. At least Canadian reporters were more respectful to Roberta than their counterparts in the U.S. had been to Sally Ride. She had once been asked whether she was planning to wear a bra in zero gravity.

Roberta realized, whether she liked it or not, she was now a spokesperson and an albeit reluctant role model. She chose her words carefully. "I have no problem with affirmative action at the lower levels, where women need to be given opportunities to gain knowledge and experience. Once you have reached a certain level of achievement in your field, there is no room for that. It would be foolish to make such important assignments on the basis of sex. There is too much at stake."

Roberta warmed up in her many subsequent interviews and speeches. "When the opportunity came up, I thought gee, this is really exciting. This is Canadian history in the making and wouldn't it be wonderful to be able to be part of this? Even if I didn't get to fly, to be in this group of people ... maybe do real science up there would be so exciting." The normally serious and scientifically focused Roberta turned out to be good at this first part of her new job — public relations for the Canadian space industry. She was in big demand. Her bosses christened her "Roberta Glenn" after her effusively positive and popular predecessor, John Glenn, the first American astronaut to orbit Earth.

With the news out officially, Roberta's parents found themselves deluged with unfamiliar attention. People in Sault Ste. Marie now said hello to Edward, even if they had never met. Mildred had to deal with all sorts of new friends, as well as family requests to have Roberta do something or appear somewhere. But Roberta would be too busy for a while to even see much of her family. She had to report for astronaut training early in the new year.

Chapter 4
The First to Fly

hen the Select Six arrived to take up their positions in Ottawa early in 1984, they crammed into a small anonymous office at the National Research Council. A shared coffeemaker in the corner sported a sign above it reminding them all to contribute to the coffee fund. There was going to be no hero worshipping here.

Assigned in teams with one medical specialist and one engineer per team, the astronaut-scientists were divided into three groups and set up face-to-face desks in tiny cubicles. Roberta was partnered with Marc Garneau, the naval commander with a PhD in engineering.

What did the astronauts really know about their new

job? They knew it was a two-year commitment at that time. The six astronauts-to-be were all scientists and had to help develop two sets of experiments — in life sciences (in Roberta's case) or in space robotics. Two of them could expect to fly as payload specialists in late 1985 or early 1986, while the others would serve as backups. If any of them was selected for a flight, they would carry out and assess the on-board experiments. They also had to be ready to take on the role of mission specialist, if ever made available by NASA. For all this, they would earn between $35,000 and $55,000 annually.

The new colleagues didn't have much time to get to know each other better before the pace quickened dramatically. Late in January, not even a month after their appointments, the NRC received a surprise invitation. NASA was offering to send a Canadian payload specialist on a shuttle scheduled for October that year — more than one year earlier than expected. The Canadian government accepted the prestigious invitation without consulting its brand-new employees — the offer was just too good to pass up. This flight would mark the first time NASA included an astronaut from another country's space program. (Ulf Merbold was a German citizen but had been trained within the NASA system as a payload specialist.) Space Transportation System (STS) 51-A was promptly nicknamed "51 eh?" to honour the inaugural Canadian presence.

The challenge for the NRC was huge — could Canada choose and train a new recruit in only nine short months?

Although NASA astronauts train for years for their flights, the Canadian payload specialists originally expected to concentrate their training within just 18 months. Now this period had been halved. But the future of all Canadian — and perhaps all non-American — astronauts was on the line.

As well, within that timeframe, the NRC had to decide on appropriate science experiments the payload specialist would supervise, then set up the protocols and related training. After all, the science was supposed to be the whole point of the flight. Fortunately, the NRC had an extremely qualified and ambitious crew of astronaut-scientists. The crew would have to jell quickly and train hard. But each wanted to be the first Canadian scientist in space. Who would be the chosen one?

Getting Sick

After condensed orientation and planning sessions, the first real astronaut training was scheduled for March. The astronauts travelled to the lab of one of the 19 finalists, Dr. Doug Watt, at McGill University in Montreal, where they rode a prototype of his "space sled." Blindfolded and wearing earplugs, the astronauts rode back and forth on a track. The device tested the effects of motion of the body's balancing system on the inner ear and was being considered as an on-board experiment.

Next they went to fellow astronaut Ken Money's lab in Toronto to further evaluate their susceptibility to motion sickness. Space sickness is a serious issue for astronauts. Productivity in space can be severely hampered by the inevitable adjustments to microgravity. A full 40 percent of astronauts admit to getting sick within 72 hours of liftoff. One of the two major tenets of Canada's space science research program — and Roberta's area of expertise — was to investigate this phenomenon and determine methods to counteract the effects.

In Ken's lab, one of the infamous diabolical spinning machines that deliberately made the astronauts throw up in the name of science was called the PAM, short for precision angular mover. Roberta gamely took her turn to be strapped in and tumbled backward in the enclosed Ferris wheel–like ride. As instructed, she started to count backward from 1000 by twos, all the while monitored by a camera that projected her progress to viewers outside. Soon after starting, she lost track of where she was in the counting, more preoccupied — like the rest of her colleagues — with trying not to vomit. When she emerged from the PAM after 10 minutes, clearly uncomfortable, Roberta asked the operator, "What? Am I pale? Am I losing my mascara?" By still being able to joke in her nauseated state, she was clearly demonstrating her self-control — the right stuff? At least she had survived longer than her desk-mate, Marc Garneau. He could only say, "Now you all know what normal performance is" before rushing to the nearest washroom.

In the same lab, the astronauts were also "lucky"

enough to experience another midway ride — a high-altitude chamber that created explosive decompression. Used to train military jet pilots in coping with the dangers of unpressurized flight without oxygen, this exercise was to prepare the astronauts for upcoming rides in NASA's zero-gravity plane. Dubbed the Weightless Wonder or the Vomit Comet, the KC-135 flies a roller coaster pattern of climbs and dives to produce 20- to 30-second periods of weightlessness as it goes over the top. At first, astronauts in training had to move slowly to get used to the sensations on board, but those with less motion susceptibility could play Superman and flip and fly through the cabin. Bob Thirsk joked it was a great way to practice breakdancing.

"Someone has to be first"

Roberta thus encountered her first sensations of space since the imaginary flights of her childhood. But it wasn't all fun. Even though the intense selection process was behind them, the candidates felt they were being assessed all over again in this new competition for the first flight. All astronauts had reason to feel performance anxiety, even if they didn't admit it. They knew susceptibility to motion sickness might not be a deciding factor, but the ability to work in spite of it could be. Who would be the best one to fly first? Who would be backup?

Despite the stresses of this internal contest, the astronauts continued to develop strong camaraderie. They supported and tried to protect one another from the more unwelcome intrusions of media and other demands. Roberta was forced to get an unlisted telephone number to protect the little privacy she had left. To keep herself centred, she decorated her cubicle with a photograph of her parents and a poster of a female astronaut floating weightless. She also sought refuge with her colleagues. In the few off hours they had, several of them worked on their flying skills in a small Cessna 172 they had bought together. Even though Roberta had had her licence for more than 15 years, she happily shared in the ownership and the instruction of others ... when she had time.

On March 13, 1984, the astronauts would find out who among them would be the first to fly. In the meantime, they devised a complicated odds game to guess by secret ballot who would be selected as the prime and who would be back-up. The astronauts' choice would have to buy the first round of drinks at the evening's celebration. The NRC's official choice would be presented with the dinner bill. Would it be the same person?

Before they had time to finish their game, however, the announcement was made during a weekly staff meeting. Marc Garneau would be the designated astronaut for Canada's first shuttle trip to space. Robert Thirsk had been selected as backup. Roberta and the rest of the group had to be envious. But they were also thrilled for their colleagues. Realizing the incredible rush and high pressure of the first flight, some of them had perhaps secretly hoped they would not be the guinea pig. They would rather look forward to a later mission, once some of the bugs were worked out.

After champagne was uncorked, another briefing followed, this one on how to deal with inevitable questions at the press conference the next day. While the six had been chosen in part for their skills in public relations, this was to be a major test for their competitive, high-achieving personalities. The questions they would face could be blunt: Why were or weren't you chosen? For Marc, Is this a culmination of a personal dream? What does it mean to Canada? The rest of them had to prepare for harder questions: Are you disappointed? Browned off? The question the only female astronaut candidate expected was, Do you think they take you seriously? Roberta wanted to groan. Each astronaut not chosen could quite honestly express optimism that he or she would be getting another chance soon. The next two flights were expected within two years.

After the announcement, the astronauts inaugurated what they hoped would be a new tradition. The celebratory dinner at one of Ottawa's fanciest restaurants was paid for by the "lucky one." The mood at dinner was collegial and merry. Roberta, Steve, Ken, and Bjarni realized they could catch their breath for a short while. The pilots in the group that night joked that Marc would likely fly in the shuttle before he had the chance to fly their Cessna solo. For Marc, there would be no relaxation after this night. There was so little time and so much to do!

At the press conference the next day, Marc modestly acknowledged his bilingual advantage and pointed out, "Someone has to be first." But from that moment, Marc ceased to be a private person. "I am a celebrity," he said to his father, "and I haven't done anything yet!"

Marc would not feel singled out all the time. Not only did he have his backup, Bob, with whom to train, he was accompanied by Roberta and the other astronauts for some of the preliminary instruction. One of the first things the group did was tour the Kennedy Space Center: Mission Control, the simulators and full-size mockups of the shuttle. After learning the basics, Roberta and the rest of the astronauts left Marc and Bob and returned to Canada to work on the experiments that would accompany Marc.

In late June, four of them were scheduled to witness a shuttle launch. Unfortunately, STS 41-D was aborted in the last six seconds, but fortunately — it seemed to the Canadian observers at least — it demonstrated that the safety systems had worked. The close call reminded everyone how extraordinary, and risky, travelling into space still was. In the end, the 41-D shuttle was delayed two months. The next — and 13th — shuttle to go would be Marc's 41-G. (It was no longer 51-A because it had moved up in the list.)

Marc Soars

Because this shuttle mission was to be a test case for foreign payload specialists, Marc had to be on his toes. NASA astronauts were not yet used to foreign astronauts or payload specialists/scientists, whom they didn't consider real astronauts in their macho test pilot–dominated world. Some viewed these pseudo-astronauts as jumping the queue that they themselves had stood in a long time, waiting for a flight.

Marc was aware and understanding of the ambivalence toward him. For his part, he compared his task to sprinting in a marathon. But he and the rest of the Canadian astronauts were determined to be as adaptable and flexible as ambassadors. As he shuttled back and forth from Canada to the space shuttle simulator at Johnson Space Center in Houston, attending lectures, demonstrations, and simulations, he kept Roberta and the rest in the loop so they would be better prepared when their turn came. Marc's diplomatic efforts paid off. He and Bob were invited to use the NASA astronauts' private gym, an honour usually accorded only "real" astronauts. Garneau had made the grade.

On October 5, 1984, Dr. Marc Garneau became the first Canadian to fly in space as he and the rest of the seven-member crew blasted off in *Challenger*. He had been an astronaut for only nine months. Roberta was there to watch, learn, and act as a live commentator for Canadian TV. "I bet Marc is saying, 'What a ride, what a ride!'" she told viewers as *Challenger* left Earth. She took her parents to Florida to watch, too, to prepare them for what she hoped would be a flight of her own soon.

When Marc returned to Earth on October 13, Roberta was on site again in another official capacity: she was one of the team of scientists and doctors who greeted then tested Marc to find out the effects of the trip on his body. In the end, both NASA and Canada were delighted with Marc's mission — it set the standard for how a payload specialist flight should be flown and paved the way for more Canadians on board future shuttles.

After his return, Marc was in high demand all over Canada. Over a few months, he made 230 appearances. Bob handled another 120. More surprising were the requests for another astronaut. Even though she hadn't yet flown, Roberta was third in demand with 65 appearances! Canadians were indeed interested in the space program, and Roberta responded to the spotlight. With her gift for explaining scientific subjects simply and sharing her excitement about space, she was a boon for the space industry.

Who's Next?
But there was really no time to relax and reflect after Marc returned from space. It was back to training for the six. The two missions originally planned for the following year might occur only two months apart, so there was lots to do. One of Roberta's jobs was to head the life sciences committee to examine possibilities for science and medicine in space, even a mini-hospital for the newly announced International Space Station. She still didn't know whether she would be carrying

out experiments on the next flight. That decision had to be delayed as the flights were pushed back in the schedule.

In December 1985, the next Canadian astronaut was finally disclosed. Once again, Roberta was not chosen. The flight, planned now for March 1987, would concentrate not on life sciences, but on the second component of the Canadian space science focus — space robotics. Because this was Steve MacLean's specialty, he was assigned, with fellow engineer Bjarni Tryggvason as backup. This time, it was Steve who was presented with the outrageous bill at the celebratory dinner.

The others could not help but focus their hopes on the next flight, which was expected to be announced very soon. The life sciences flight would logically be next to go, but there were no guarantees. Roberta knew she would have to be patient and wait for the next flight announcement — and, she hoped, her turn.

Chapter 5
Disaster!

ot even two months after Steve had been selected, the worst possible thing happened. Frustrating delays had been slowing the lineup of shuttles waiting their turn in the launch sequence, but January 28, 1986, was the date scheduled for *Challenger* to fly. There had already been seven postponements of this one flight, so the pressure was even greater to get it launched and get the shuttle program back on track.

The day began chilly, with the temperature hovering around the freezing point. As it had nine times previously in the past, *Challenger* did successfully lift off that day. However, before the cheering had died down — 73 seconds into the flight — an enormous flash fire of exploding hydrogen and oxygen lit up the sky. The shuttle had been travelling at 318 km/h before it blew up. Flaming debris, white streamers of smoke, and condensed ice particles rained down for almost an hour onto the Atlantic Ocean. The cause of the explosion was a mechanical malfunction. A rubber O-ring seal, used to seal the space between segments of the solid rocket boosters, leaked because it was too cold and therefore too brittle. The liquid fuel tank exploded and all seven crew members — including the first civilian on board a shuttle — lost their lives.

In Ottawa that day, Roberta went bouncing into the astronaut office, full of enthusiasm from a meeting in which funding for one of the life sciences experiments had been approved. Ken had the radio on and, right before the phone started ringing off the hook, relayed the grim news.

"I just went into a cold sweat when I heard. I felt my stomach turn. I had sweat rolling down my armpits into my hands," Roberta recalled. She couldn't help but think of her colleagues who had just died, years of life yet to give. It also brought back the recent loss of her father, who had unexpectedly died from a heart attack two months earlier. His death was particularly hard on Roberta — her father had always been one of her great boosters. Roberta went home glumly to watch the unfolding coverage on TV. She and Ken were advised not to comment to the press, but both were acutely aware of how their own futures were now in jeopardy.

The disaster suspended shuttle flights indefinitely. After

building on 25 years of steady gains and finally picking up serious momentum, with a new generation of people even starting to think of living and working in space as a given, the manned space program stopped.

In Limbo

Two years of serious soul-searching followed for Roberta and all the astronauts. They felt as if they were in limbo along with the shuttle program. If NASA did relaunch the program, it might prefer to fly only its own career astronauts and not risk the lives of civilians or non-career astronauts, especially payload specialists from a foreign country. "I had to regroup my thoughts," recalled Roberta. She didn't really know what was possible in her future. To interviewers, her comment was, "This is not the be-all and end-all to my life."

Roberta realized she might never go up in space, and maybe that was okay. She acknowledged that what they had learned from the *Challenger* disaster would make the whole process safer for space travel, but it was still a high-risk, experimental undertaking. Her contract with the NRC had been extended, but it was up to her to accept the uncertainty. However, after many discussions with her colleagues and bosses about how the Astronaut Program had to change, she decided she would not be swayed in her commitment. After all, NASA missions were expensive and depended on payloads such as scientific experiments funded by other countries. Roberta knew at least unofficially that she was still a candidate for the next life sciences flight if shuttles resumed. There was still hope.

Filling the Time

In the meantime, the question for Roberta and the other astronauts was, as Marc Garneau expressed it, "How do we occupy our time in a useful manner?" With no flights on the horizon, they had less to do or at least more time to do it. Because the demands of their workload until now had meant they'd risked becoming out of date in rapidly changing technical fields, some became more active in their respective fields of engineering and science. Instead of training on the shuttle as she planned, Roberta carried on with other kinds of training. She didn't want to lose her hard-earned clinical or research skills, so she returned part-time to another of her passions — medicine — to get her through the waiting period.

The uncertainties of the space program had reminded Roberta that she shouldn't neglect the rest of her life. She consequently looked for "stepping stones that would leave doors open" after space. In 1988, she joined the staff at Sunnybrook Medical Centre and the Toronto General Hospital in Toronto. At this critical time in her career, she became involved in science experiments of her own to fill gaps in her experience. The medical aspects of future space travel and their clinical spinoffs still fascinated her, and being an astronaut gave her access to research that she probably would not have had otherwise.

Disaster!

In her "spare time," Roberta worked in microgravity. She did experiments on NASA's KC-135 aircraft to measure blood flow to the brain during weightlessness. She knew her work could be useful to both space science and stroke research. Plus, returning to her research as a neurologist may have compensated for the frustration she felt by the interruption in her space career.

As chairperson of the life sciences subcommittee of the NRC's space division, Roberta worked all over the world for the better part of a year. She travelled to Europe, the former Soviet Union, and Japan to compare notes with other scientists.

Roberta maintained her routine to stay in top physical condition. When at home — now Ottawa — she worked out at least 20 minutes a day and swam three times a week in the pool in her apartment block. When NASA decided it wanted to fly shuttles again, she wanted to be ready. She put off for later her other hobbies of refinishing furniture and gardening. As often as she was able, she returned to Sault Ste. Marie to visit her mother, other family, and friends.

While NASA was still ruminating over its shuttle disaster and the future of its space program, the Soviets continued to make breakthroughs. Cosmonauts proved they could live in space for more than a year. Fortunately, cooperation rather than competition between the former Cold War enemies had become more routine since the early 1970s, when the struggle for national superiority was replaced by the search for more peaceful uses of space, such as scientific study. Soviets had even flown U.S. experiments on their biosatellites (manned by monkeys) when NASA's shuttle program was only in its design phase. This cooperation facilitated the exchange of scientific and technological expertise at a shared cost.

The Americans were not content to allow the Soviets to have space to themselves, however — and Canada was also eager to establish its presence more firmly in the space race. After a moratorium of two years, the shuttle program resumed in 1988. In 1989, the Canadian Astronaut Program became part of the newly established independent government agency, the Canadian Space Agency (CSA). This was a sign Canada was becoming even more serious about its role in space and its future partnership with other space-going nations.

Back on the Campaign Trail

The next year, the CSA announced that a flight was expected in 1990. Either Roberta or Ken was expected to fly on this flight since it was designated for life sciences research. Roberta dropped all her extracurricular work and concentrated only on getting the nod. And as Bob Thirsk observed, "When Roberta focuses on a task, she's hell bent." She still saw a chance to fulfil a life-long dream.

After the hiatus, however, the circumstances of the flight had changed. Instead of a regular mid-deck flight, where science experiments were restricted to the shuttle's tiny living quarters, the science would be the main payload. This first flight of the International Microgravity Lab (IML) was the collaboration of six space agencies, including Canada's, that was preparing a unique pre-fabricated laboratory for the shuttle's cargo bay — the first real lab in space. It was now not just up to Canada to designate the scientist who would fly. Because of the involvement of six space agencies, the selection had to be made by all the agencies' scientists.

Each scientist was working on a possible research project for space. This campaigning for the job did not come naturally to Roberta. She wanted to be recognized for her credentials — with a broader base of diverse science, she was confident she'd be considered the most qualified candidate. However, Roberta said she would quit if she was selected because of her gender ... and she wasn't joking.

On January 20, 1990, the newspaper announced that the CSA and NASA concurred with the scientists who had been polled by secret ballot — Roberta would be the scientist-astronaut to oversee their experiments on board. The experienced Ken Money would serve as her backup. They also learned that their flight, STS-42, had been moved ahead of Steve MacLean's, which was originally scheduled to go in 1987 after *Challenger*. It had been almost six years since Marc Garneau flew the first and only mission for Canada.

In spite of the long wait, Roberta was delighted that she was going to be the second Canadian to fly. Fortunately, Ken agreed that she indeed had "extraordinary amounts of the right stuff." Despite these endorsements, the inevitable personal questions about her gender still had to be endured. This time, the questions were about Roberta's potential for motherhood. Now in her mid-40s, had she sacrificed her child-bearing years while waiting for her turn to fly? Although she knew having a family would have jeopardized her astronaut career, Roberta tried hard not to be fazed by it all. She responded that children were not to be part of her "biological contribution to society." She had other plans.

Chapter 6
Astronauts in Training

y 1990, Roberta had spent six years in the Astronaut Program. She couldn't be blamed for feeling like a flightless kiwi bird. Most of her training had been on the ground. For some of that time, she didn't even know whether she — or any of her fellow astronaut candidates — would ever fly. Now in the lineup, she was determined to be the best she could be. She kept working hard, filling in gaps in her knowledge and experience to counteract potential naysayers. Accustomed as Roberta was to roadblocks, she liked to be prepared. "I wanted to be as qualified as possible, so if people didn't want me, they'd have to say: 'Look, you're a woman and I don't think you can do it.'" Her toughness was by now well established. It

Roberta during training in a T-33 jet

had to be for what she would face over the next couple of years — the most intensive training period of her life. At least she wouldn't have to do it alone. She and Ken would be tackling it together.

Ken Money

If Roberta emulated John Glenn's behaviour, Ken was his lookalike. As the oldest Canadian astronaut, Ken had dreamed of going into space since 1958, when he started working in the space science field — and Roberta was barely a teenager. Since 1962, he had been consulting for NASA as a vestibular physiologist specializing in the inner ear and motion sickness. A pilot and parachutist, he had applied to NASA's astronaut program directly, but had not made the final cut in two tries. When the Canadian program began, he naturally assumed he would have a head start. And even when the National Research Council decided to open up the competition, in part as a public relations exercise, Ken still believed he would rise to the top of the applicants' pile.

Now Ken was finally assigned to a mission, but it was as backup. If he was disappointed, he did not show it publicly. His first allegiance, he knew, had to be to the science and the experiments they would prepare for the mission. He prepared as intensely as Roberta. Having worked with NASA for some time, he was of enormous help in facilitating both their adjustments to NASA's systems.

Teammates

The payload specialists of STS-42 and their backups started working together months before their flight date, first scheduled for December 1990. Their training was expected to take up to 18 months but lasted even longer because the flight was delayed many times. Roberta and Ken in particular maintained a phenomenal training schedule between the NASA centres in Houston, Texas, and Huntsville, Alabama. For two years, they flew between these bases on commercial airlines at least once, more often twice a week.

Travelling was the most tiring aspect of the whole

process for Roberta. She spent hours in planes, and many days and nights in airports, admitting that the schedule they kept was possible only because neither she nor Ken had young children. During the training, she virtually had to make her home in the U.S., but bringing special items along, such as Canadian carvings, helped lower the stress of being away from her real home for so long.

At the Johnson Space Center in Houston, just like Marc and Bob before them, Roberta and Ken learned how to work on the orbiter and familiarized themselves with the computers and software she would be using in space. Many things had changed since Marc's flight. Bailout training, for example, was one of the more than 200 changes to shuttle hardware and software due to the *Challenger* accident. At the Marshall Space Flight Center in Huntsville, they set up and worked on the scientific experiments for which she would be responsible. Roberta had to practise the experiments over and over, since in space, she would have only one chance to get them right.

When she wasn't travelling, Roberta put in long days. She would typically get up around 6:00 a.m., exercise for an hour (usually with ankle weights to keep her heart strong), then work for 12 to 14 hours. Every day brought a large stack of mail to deal with, as well as NASA manuals to absorb and speeches to prepare. Roberta would get hungry every two hours, but often had no chance to take a break. She carried a bag of snacks for when there was no time for meals.

By late 1990, the rest of the crew had been assigned. Commander of Roberta's flight was 46-year-old Ron Grabe. He was no stranger to the command role, having been a colonel in the U.S. Air Force. He also had been a combat fighter pilot, test pilot, and test pilot instructor and had an engineering science background. This would be his third shuttle flight. Second-in-command and pilot Steve Oswald and flight engineer Bill Readdy, both naval aviators and test pilots, were rookies on the shuttle. The mission specialists were both veterans and doctors — Sonny Carter and Norm Thagard. Norm was also an engineer and came from the Marines. The other payload specialist was second-timer Ulf Merbold, from the European Space Agency. Both he and Roberta would conduct experiments in physics and life sciences.

The year before the scheduled liftoff, which was now expected in fall 1991, was the most intense. Beginning early in the year, Roberta simulated — in minute detail — life and work aboard a shuttle with the rest of the crew. They would not have the luxury of time to adjust in space itself. Every minute would be accounted for, and most of the mission's ten precious days would have to be productive. For eight months, Roberta and the six other astronauts developed a tight bond. The many delays added a common obstacle that forged their team. Living and working in such close quarters, they learned to respect one another's strengths and weaknesses. Their lives would truly depend on their teamwork, both in training and ultimately in any emergency in flight.

Tragedy hit prematurely when Sonny was killed in a commercial airline accident en route to give a speech for a local community group in Brunswick, Georgia. The crew found themselves as shocked and saddened as if a family member had passed away. A seasoned veteran of space flight, Sonny had been a breath of fresh air to the team, always sharing his light-hearted enthusiasm. The rest of the crew drew even closer together, feeling his loss, but they had to continue their preparations. Three-time veteran Dave Hilmers joined the group in place of Sonny.

Simulating Emergencies

The astronauts' training was tailored to each person's task, so Roberta didn't have to practise flying the shuttle, even though, as a pilot, she might have liked to. Payload specialists were required to learn enough about the shuttlecraft, especially the launch, landing, and safety systems, in case of emergency. With practically every minute accounted for, Roberta had little free time for her own flying during mission training, but she did manage a little hot air ballooning for landform recognition practice.

Nonetheless, having a pilot's licence did prove helpful in getting along with the rest of the crew. Most NASA astronauts had military pilot backgrounds, and much of the technical language at NASA derived from aviation, so Roberta could understand the lingo and the jokes. Training as a pilot had also prepared her for thinking "quickly under very tight periods of time when you're enclosed and you have to be thinking about a number of things at once." She was familiar with functioning upside down and under the pressure of G forces.

Although the new crew hoped they would never have to use emergency procedures, they reviewed them regularly. They learned how to fight fires on the runway, progressing from spraying a small contained fire with hand-held extinguishers to teaming up on a long hose to douse an enormous blaze. Both sporting big Canadian flags on their flight suits, Ken and Roberta spiritedly cheered each other and their other teammates on. "Atta girl!" "Nice job, fireman!" On the day of the launch, the reality was that the astronauts would be the only ones left to deal with any such fires. Everybody else would safely be several kilometres away.

Roberta and her crew even practised the unlikely sequence of escaping a hypothetical fire during the launch. From the launch tower, they were supposed to jump into baskets for a "rapid egress" down a steep wire. The ever-adventurous Roberta thought it could have been great fun if it did not evoke worries about the most dangerous part of the trip. The final aspect of emergency training was indeed fun — they all took turns driving an emergency vehicle that was actually a tank powerful enough to blast through a fence.

During all this emergency training, the astronaut crew tried not to dwell on its solemnity. While discussing an orbiter bailout scenario, the instructor pointed out that the life raft would work in saltwater only. Roberta laughed, commenting that they'd better avoid the Great Lakes then.

Simulating Life On Board

One of the most useful parts in training was the simulation of work in a weightless environment. Toiling in scuba gear in a wet facility, or pool, was the closest they could get. A keen swimmer, Roberta usually looked forward to the pool time. One day, however, she was running a temperature of 39°C, but the schedule was so rigid, she dared not beg off sick. Limp and already overheated, Roberta pulled on her long wool underwear and wool socks, then struggled into the orange flight suit. After she was helped into a parachute harness, fighting nausea, she was dropped unceremoniously from a hoist above the pool.

There were several tasks to accomplish in the water that day. One was to swim — or at least struggle — to a partially inflated life raft, climb in, and bail it out. Another had her slowly drag a full parachute canopy over her head in the water, hand by hand, without panicking. Finally, she had to demonstrate proficiency in an emergency exit of the orbiter by somersaulting from the mockup hatch a couple of metres into the pool. Her helmet filled with water. When she had successfully dealt with that problem, she had to give the A-OK sign to the poolside staff, who were jokingly rating each astronaut. "Six and a half," one remarked. With the little energy she had left, Roberta could still jest, "How 'bout it, guys? Olympics next?"

After one pool session, Roberta realized how much it would help if her reactions to these emergency procedures were automatic. She decided to take scuba diving even more seriously and signed up for extra training. Among all the other demands of the mission training, Roberta earned her scuba certificate.

The only gap Roberta noticed in her training was that there were far too few sessions combining photography with geography and geology for her liking. As the shuttle orbited, Earth rotated and she wanted to be able to identify quickly what she was seeing before the image was lost. Although she had been told by other seasoned astronauts there would be limited time and opportunity to set up photos on board, Roberta, ever the photographer, planned to take many pictures of her favourite places from above.

Even the creature comforts weren't overlooked. While John Glenn and other early astronauts used to have to rely on tasteless freeze-dried rations, astronauts could now eat almost anything in space, unless it required refrigeration. Roberta and each astronaut were able to sample, rate, and choose each and every item for meals. The only stipulation was that the meals had to meet the required caloric intake value so the astronauts could keep their energy up. Roberta favoured meals such as chicken and veggies and shrimp cocktail, and snacks like cashews and dehydrated strawberries.

Tortillas replaced bread because they were less likely to make crumbs, which could cause problems if they floated around the shuttle. "I'm going to look like a tortilla when I come down," she kidded to her colleagues.

Of the few personal belongings she was allowed on the shuttle, Roberta chose to bring more food — Girl Guide cookies and maple candies. Also along for the ride were her dad's space shuttle tie and a piece of the hot air balloon that she had flown. She planned to bring it back to her ballooning club to boast that it was the highest flying balloon ever.

Simulating Science

All through the specialized training, Roberta kept up with her scientific preparations. The International Microgravity Lab was the mission payload, the main reason for the shuttle going up. It was considered critical preparation for the permanent space lab envisioned for the International Space Station. The unique lab was the closest thing so far to a real lab in which scientists could work in space. A complex system of twelve racks was set up as a small lab module that would be encased in protective shielding in the shuttle's payload bay. One rack, called a Biorack, was the size of a broom closet and contained the laboratory components for all the biology experiments. For the first time, the scientists on board would not have to work in the crowded mid-deck and could be ready to be productive almost as soon as the shuttle reached its orbit altitude.

Roberta was going to be the surrogate scientist for many experiments. She would be working on behalf of more than 200 scientists, teams led by principal investigators from the ground. To fully understand all of the science, she had travelled to every lab of every principal investigator of each experiment, all over the world. One trip to Europe lasted five weeks and had 14 sub-trips. She and Ken checked on the original experiments and samples and tried out all the equipment. The IML Spacelab simulator in Houston was then set up to simulate everything that could be expected in space — except microgravity — and the payload specialists practised the experiments over and over. They knew they would have only one chance to get them right in space.

One day, the scientists were testing an experiment code named SLIME in the lab. Like everything in the space program, the code name was an acronym, but it also referred to the nature of the material. Joking that the slime mould belonged in a horror movie, Roberta and her colleagues could agree on one thing: no one really knew how slime would behave in microgravity. After all, that's why they were going to space.

Final Rehearsal
In June 1991, Roberta decided to move from Ottawa to Houston, anticipating her flight's imminent departure. But continual delays in the launch date meant she questioned the decision frequently. Moving was stressful though, and she

had enough on her plate to keep her busy. Roberta, like each of the astronauts, found herself worrying about little things, such as breaking an ankle in the last few months. After all the training, at this stage, no one wanted to miss out on the flight.

In October, the final dress rehearsal was in Houston on the shuttle mockup. The crew simulated living and working on the shuttle for one last time before they would do it for real. One day during rehearsal, Roberta must have thought she was in an episode of *Star Trek* as she found herself unexpectedly battling an "alien" visitor to the lab. Over the speaker system that was supposed to simulate ground to air communications, she hypothesized it was a mutant escapee from one of the fruit fly experiments. With help and a high-tech weapon — a broom — the scientists trapped the yellow-jacketed invader and held it up to the recording camera. The alien was a wasp. "Just another sting operation," someone quipped. Soon after, all preparations were finalized and the Spacelab was ready to be loaded into the payload bay for flight.

Roberta was ready, too, but still waiting for confirmation of the launch date. "Each time a shuttle went up I thought, I'm one more closer to the pad." Six shuttles had launched in the last year, but which shuttle would she fly in? *Columbia* was originally designated for Roberta's 10-day flight, but it was taken out of service in 1991 to be refit for longer flights. *Discovery* was then expected to fly the Spacelab. But since it was designed for 7-day missions, the mission had to be shortened to 7 days — to Roberta's great dismay.

After its last flight, which landed in California, *Discovery* was piggybacked on a Boeing 747 and flown to Cape Canaveral to prepare for its 14th launch. On December 19, *Discovery* was rolled out to the launch pad, but another month would go by before it would be ready to lift off. Since its first postponement December 6, 1990, this mission had been delayed 19 times. But anyone who had spent as many years in postgraduate studies and as an astronaut-in-waiting as Roberta knew about patience and delayed gratification.

Two weeks before launch, the astronauts finally flew into Florida in their T-38 trainer planes. They didn't want to go anywhere else but space at this point. The back-to-back interviews just prior to the latest revised launch day of January 22, 1992, managed to subdue even the energetic and enthusiastic Roberta. She was getting tired of answering speculative questions. She just wanted to get up there, even if it was going to be mainly hard work and little time to wonder at it all. "If they don't give me time [to look out the window], I'll have to go to the bathroom a lot," she grinned wearily.

Chapter 7
Liftoff!

he United Nations had optimistically endorsed 1992 as the International Year of Space. But after so many postponements of her flight the year before, Roberta had often wondered if she would ever leave Earth. When she finally did, she would be carrying a heavy load. "With her, go our future dreams for the space program and science community," CBC commentator Peter Mansbridge remarked to Marc Garneau while waiting for the launch the morning of January 22, 1992.

Discovery, the most experienced space shuttle, was once again sitting on Pad 39A, its silhouette against the Florida sky dwarfing the surroundings. There had been yet another delay early that morning. The ultra-sensitive weather sensors had interpreted some minor ground fog as potential for a thunderstorm. Shuttle watchers knew that even the slightest drizzle could critically damage the shuttle's heat-resistant tiles when the shuttle rocketed into the sky. And if the winds were even a little gusty, they could make an emergency landing impossible. If anything at all went wrong after the launch — even after the booster rockets and fuel tank were dropped — the pilots were expected to RTLS, return to the launch site. *Challenger* was still too fresh in people's minds for NASA to take any chances.

After 45 launches, the team at Kennedy Space Center was certainly experienced. Their series of elaborate tests and inspections included a computer scan of every inch and an icicle check, despite the almost perfect weather. An hour later than the last scheduled liftoff time, everything was ready once more for countdown.

Meanwhile, the astronauts had been getting ready to launch, too. The normal pre-flight jitters were starting to show. Like all the astronauts before her, even the normally cool Roberta must have faced some of the usual doubts: Am I really good enough? Trained enough? Will I make a mistake? After all, Roberta had experienced only simulations so far, and, as happens in simulations, had "died" many times. But she had pronounced herself as psychologically fit and prepared to fly as she could be, reassuring reporters and her family, "There's a game plan to deal with every emergency." Privately though, she wondered, could anyone *really* feel prepared for a rocket launch?

Roberta and the crew had been secluded for a week — not only to solidify their team bond but also to prevent them from getting sick. Only primary contacts — in Roberta's case, her sister, Barbara — were allowed brief visits, and not before they had been thoroughly checked by the doctors to ensure they weren't carrying germs. In space, bacteria could grow larger and faster and were often resistant to antibiotics. Since a bacterial infection could show up in a week, both the doctor and astronaut in Roberta had to agree the seven-day quarantine period was reasonable. She certainly didn't want to jeopardize all her careful preparations by getting a cold at the last minute. It wouldn't be hard to get sick, given the schedule she'd been keeping.

Launch Prep

On launch day, the crew was up at 4:00 a.m. for the traditional pre-launch breakfast. As they cut the cake iced with a replica of the STS-42 mission patch, their inside jokes kept everyone's mood light. Fortunately, only the NASA cameraperson, not the usual media pack, was there to record their final Earthbound pre-flight hours.

By 6:30 a.m., Roberta was in the "clean" room of the astronauts' quarantined quarters getting dressed. The process took about an hour and a half: first came the diaper, then the long underwear, the gravity pants, socks, and boots. Then she added the flotation device and the signalling device that were also part of the suit. The whole thing added almost another 90 pounds to her weight. The launch and re-entry suit was supposed to protect against heat and pressure changes during liftoff, and cold or fire, in case of emergency. Despite the inflatable lower back pad and seat support, Roberta had heard the suit would not be comfortable while she was on her back for the four hours before liftoff.

It was still not dawn. Dressed in their bulky orange suits covered in the multicoloured NASA and Canadian Space Agency mission patches they had helped design, the crew performed the traditional dramatic walk out to the van. Only reporters with special passes were present to record the event, but the broadcast would reach the astronauts' anxious families as well as the rest of the world later on newscasts. Roberta had been telling reporters earlier how much she looked forward to this day. "The most fun is the reaction of my family and friends. They are so excited and so proud."

Among her still sleepy crewmates, Roberta was easily the most animated, grinning wildly and raising both hands. "Yes! Yes! Yes!" she called out to the cameras. This was her way of sending a message to her 65 friends and family members who were gathering in a private viewing area about 5 kilometres from the launch site. "I wanted them to know I was all right, to relieve their anxiety a bit — that this was going to be a lot of fun …"

As she rode in the van to the launch pad, Roberta's thoughts of her family's pride turned to their unspoken fear

An official NASA photograph of Roberta dressed
in the familiar orange flight suit

of her not returning. Somberly, she rode the elevator to the
"195 Foot Level" and the white room adjoining the shuttle.
"It's impossible not to imagine that moment after you've said

goodbye to your family and you board that shuttle … you're bound to wonder if that's the last time."

The white room was the astronauts' last stop before entering the shuttle. Everything in the room, even the clothing of the NASA staff assigned to help the astronauts, was a symbolic hygienic white. Once she donned her white communication cap, Roberta looked more like Snoopy the dog than an astronaut. Her rigid helmet was then secured over her cap and onto the neck ring of the space suit by dog teeth. She was ready to board the shuttle.

Countdown

Payload Specialist One — "PS1" in NASA lingo — Roberta Bondar was strapped into place on a take-down chair on the mid-deck. She and Ulf found themselves, as in the simulation, lying on their backs with their knees pointing upward. They were firmly belted to prevent them from smashing into the floor during the ride "uphill."

Understandably, the never-still Roberta felt inhibited by all her cumbersome garb. The head gear made her feel overly large and especially restricted in her neck motion. She couldn't look out the mid-deck window because it was covered for the launch with a metal shield. She couldn't read a book in the weak green light emanating from the chem sticks. Her huge pressure gloves made it impossible to push the buttons on her microcassette recorder without it dropping. She felt "like a goldfish with an anchor." But eventually, Roberta relaxed and welcomed the luxury of time to think about all her preparation for this moment. Time to reflect had been so rare the last hectic months.

At T minus 5 minutes, the clock stopped again, this time for a final planned weather check. Listening to the update over her headset, Roberta thought about whether she would have to use the bailout training. From where she was lying, she could see the emergency cue card stuck on the mid-deck locker. She had prepared for two scenarios. If an emergency occurred before liftoff, she would have to take off her parachute and lock her visor down before rolling out of the chair. Within three minutes, she would have to go through the checklist: pull the quick-disconnect lap belts, release the chute, evacuate, and slide down the wire. This was the launch pad egress she had practised not too long ago for what she hoped was the last time.

The second scenario was a bailout after launch. This time Roberta had to remember to keep her parachute on while following the rest of the cue card procedures. Would she need to use this training at all? She hoped not. She had absolutely no worries about the pilot-astronauts doing their job. "The guys driving the bus have been there and know where the buttons are."

Outside, and inside, everybody could hear the all-important countdown resume. The final weather check, shortly before 10:00 a.m., was clear. Launch minus 2 minutes and 30 seconds: Roberta put the helmet visor down and

A commemorative card celebrating the liftoff
of mission STS-42 with Roberta on board

turned her oxygen on. Then it was time to go. "We're going to
do it!" Roberta couldn't help exclaiming as the main engines
came alive.

"T-minus 10 seconds and 9, 8 ...7 ... we have a go for main engine start, we have three main engines up and running ... 3 ... 2 ...1 ... 0 and liftoff!"

With a deafening roar, the whole ship began to vibrate. The rookie astronauts had been warned that the feeling during liftoff would be like someone taking them by the shoulders and shaking them. The 4 $^{1}/_{2}$ million pound rocket was lifted from the pad by 7 million pounds of thrust.

"The shuttle has cleared the tower," came the joyous announcement shortly after. The noise and vibrations made it impossible for Roberta to think this was just another day. There was no mistaking a rocket ship for a simulator. The monster roller coaster ride up was bone jolting — more rattle and roll than she had ever experienced. As a distraction, she started to sing a song she knew well, "O Canada, our home and native land ..." Her thoughts strayed to her family again and then to her astronaut colleagues, those who had gone up before her. Everyone on board was painfully aware of how close they were flying to the sixth anniversary of the *Challenger* accident.

When the two largest rockets fell away with more commotion 2 minutes and 6 seconds after liftoff, the astronauts cheered. They'd passed a dangerous milestone. Roberta felt the pressure of two Gs (twice the force of gravity) instantaneously, then three Gs. It felt like a full-grown gorilla sitting on her chest. She could hardly move for 45 seconds.

In Orbit

Eight and a half minutes after leaving Earth, they reached 28,000 km/h, the speed necessary to break out of the atmosphere. The main engines stopped firing. Before the large external tank separated and fell away, Roberta prepared the camera for Dave Hilmers to capture it on film. The pilots fired the Orbital Maneuvering System engines to position the shuttle correctly in orbit. The shuttle was then poised, tail down, in a delicate balance almost 300 kilometres above Earth in the thermosphere, free-falling in an orbit that matched Earth's curve.

The shuttle's ride turned calm and smooth and Roberta felt instantly weightless. Surreal. "Suddenly there is no more acceleration and no more pressure on my body. It is like being at the top of a roller coaster and my whole body is in free-fall. My helmet is no longer heavy. Everything feels like it wants to float away from me, even the camera."

At last Roberta unstrapped herself from her seat and removed her launch suit. Packing away the take-down chair, she wished her space pal from long ago — Barbara — was there to share this adventure. Her stomach filled with butterflies, curiosity, and joy. Going up the ladder from the mid-deck without having to place one foot above the other felt more wonderful than she had imagined. But even that sensation was surpassed by the spectacular view from flight deck.

Roberta's first view of the planet Earth was over water. Space black replaced the blue of the sky, and she saw a thick band of fuzzy bright blue bordering the edge of Earth. Sunlight reflected from the blue waters of the Pacific, sending bright light through *Discovery*'s windows.

Roberta found the atmosphere 3-D, like in her childhood View-Master. She had to shift her gaze often to keep up with speed and the vistas. Ninety minutes after reaching space, travelling at 8 km/s, *Discovery* had already been around Earth once. Unlike on Earth, where the view ended with the horizon — 160 kilometres on a clear day — the view from space was about 2000 kilometres. Roberta had never seen something so big and was unprepared for this overwhelming emotional rendezvous with her home planet. "To see Earth from space is like meeting someone I have read about and admired for many years."

But she had to put away all the emotions for the time being. There was work to do. After all the shuttle systems were activated, Norm Thagard opened the payload bay doors to release the built-up heat. Three hours into the flight, right on schedule, Roberta headed to the one-window Spacelab to begin her experiments. She was on the "day" shift. Ulf would take the "night" shift, so he was off to try to sleep.

There was no real day or night in space — 45 minutes of light followed 45 minutes of darkness, like a film in fast forward. Instead, days were divided into blue and red shifts that corresponded to Earth's day and night. The crew members had set their biological clocks to the appropriate schedule beforehand with the help of bright lights to simulate daytime.

Half the crew had been assigned to sleep on each shift. This helped free up the small areas that they shared for sleeping and working, too. Before she started her day, Roberta had one last backward glance out the upper-deck windows. Then as she floated down the narrow 7-metre-long tunnel connecting the mid-deck to the lab, she must have wondered if she was still dreaming.

Chapter 8
Working on the Edge

n perhaps the most exciting day of her life, Roberta felt as if she was reaching the top of a roller coaster — the point where her stomach wanted to lift off. She couldn't see or think very clearly either. She was experiencing several of the typical symptoms of space sickness she knew so well as a researcher. Disorientation was to be expected in microgravity — her body's normal system of balance was confused. She had to remind herself not to move her head too quickly. Even though she knew it was inevitable and was accustomed to the drill, she was still disappointed to have to pull out the vomit bag. Roberta had so much to see and do, but joined the rest of the crew in going slow and feeling crummy that first day.

The weightless environment affected her body in other ways, too. Without gravity, there was nothing to help pump the blood and other fluids around her body. Her nasal passages became congested. Puffy face syndrome banished any wrinkles from her face. Her legs started to look skinnier — like birds' legs — because most of the fluids stayed in the upper body. Although there was really no up or down in space, some of the crew felt as if up was down as all the blood pooled in their heads. They were more comfortable if they hung by their feet, like kids on monkey bars. Roberta sometimes found herself working side by side with a colleague who was upside down! The lack of gravity also produced the most peculiar thing of all for rookies — an extra dimension. No longer were the crew all crammed onto one surface, shoulder to shoulder. Hearing voices of crewmates behind her, Roberta would turn around, but find they were not behind — but underneath — her.

Moving in a microgravity environment was something Roberta had until now been able to practise only in 30-second stints, aboard NASA's Vomit Comet. She had learned to slow down her movements because, without her body's weight holding her back, she tended to move too far or too much. Then she would overcompensate, often ending up where she didn't want to be. Her legs were essentially useless for movement. She had to use the foot restraints to anchor herself when she needed to do something; otherwise, her hands were constantly occupied. She and the other first-time astronauts gradually accustomed themselves to floating around the spaceship. Their arms hung freely in front of them, and their joints — hips, knees, and elbows — all remained in their neutral, slightly bent positions.

Roberta was experiencing first-hand all the things NASA had not been able to simulate on the ground. This was fascinating to her both as a rookie astronaut and a scientist. "Your body changes to become really a different being when you're in space." To Roberta, the biggest challenge was still adaptation to the environment. And as the payload specialist, she was there to research how to better anticipate and minimize the effects of microgravity for future astronauts.

Although the crew had prepared as well as they could have, the adjustments they had to make to the weightless and crowded environment took valuable time and effort. The most mundane tasks on Earth were challenging in microgravity. Even unpacking clothes proved to be an adventure. Roberta was not the only one who encountered an exploding locker stuffed with too much. "If you pull out one sock, everything comes out like a jack-in-the-box!" Fortunately NASA had colour-coded items to differentiate each crew member's equipment so they wouldn't spend unnecessary time sorting out which runaway item belonged to whom.

The payload crew had to keep track of more than clothes though. There were thousands of essential science items on board that could not be left unattended. Items such as notebooks or water bags did not stay in pockets or on laps

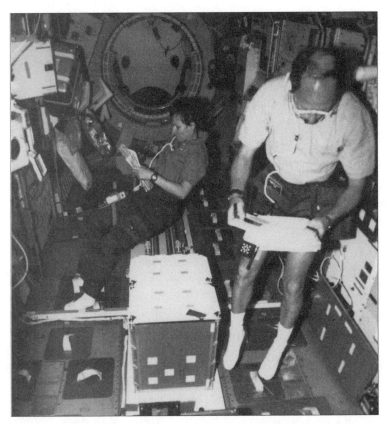

Roberta and a colleague during space flight on STS-42

unless they were fastened. "We need fly paper," Roberta commented to Mission Control one day. "We need one of those creatures from Star Wars who gobbles up trash." Everywhere on the shuttle were places with Velcro and duct tape to attach things to so they wouldn't float away. The crew had to be careful not to back into the stuff on the walls or they them-selves would stick!

The Science

The crew's work days were "timelined" in five-minute incre-ments on the Payload Crew Activity Plan (PCAP), with tasks planned out long in advance for maximum efficiency. Roberta was constantly checking to see how well the mission was proceeding according to this timeline. The scientist-astronauts were in fact trying to fit the original 10 days' worth of work into 7.

At Spacelab Payload Operations Control (SPOC), Ken "Spock" Money was the liaison between Roberta and all her resources on Earth. The expectations of all the scientists on the ground were inevitably high as they shared her intensity and pace. Whereas Norm Thagard once had to remind their excited colleagues in Houston that the astronauts were human beings, not machines, and were working under diffi-cult conditions, Ken had to regularly remind Roberta to take a break and eat some lunch during her 16-hour days.

STS-42, with the first International Microgravity Lab mission, was the most demanding scientific research mission to date. Roberta and Ulf were on board to perform or moni-tor 42 life sciences and materials experiments. The focus of the IML was on how humans, animals, plants, and materials all reacted to — and behaved in — the space environment. Roberta and her colleague planted seedlings of Canadian wheat and oats in the Biorack in an effort to find and develop efficient strains of plants that could cope with less than optimum conditions. This would prepare for future life in space. The payload specialists also monitored fruit flies, mouse kidney cells, frogs' eggs and sperm, along with the infamous slime mould, to see what happened to these other life forms in an environment of microgravity and cosmic radiation.

Roberta was naturally most excited about the potential of answering the medical questions. She had been able to include a special experiment set of her own, developed by her Canadian-U.S. research team, to study blood flow to the brain. Was the brain affected by the body's fluids shifting into different tissue spaces, as they did in astronauts' faces and legs, for example? The space sled Roberta and her colleagues had tested eight years earlier in Dr. Watt's lab was also on board to measure the part of the inner ear that senses gravity and what is normally up and down.

In her quest for answers to other medical questions, Roberta performed as both scientist and subject. In microgravity, an astronaut's balance is affected when the brain receives conflicting information from the eyes about body position and movement. And the more time astronauts spend in space, the more they rely on their eyes. If they close their eyes, they become disoriented. To observe these disorienting effects of weightlessness, Roberta was spun in the special Canadian microgravity vestibular investigations chair — once at the beginning and once at the end of the flight. A tiny camera inside her helmet recorded her eye movements for analysis later on Earth. If scientists could find a way to minimize the disorientation factor in space, they could improve astronauts' comfort and productivity.

Some of the other science experiments Roberta participated in were simpler. She had to provide urine samples after drinking water enriched with variants of the oxygen and hydrogen atoms. Energy expenditure was different in space, and the urine analysis would help scientists develop appropriate diets for the International Space Station.

The challenge for Roberta wasn't the science but conducting the science experiments successfully under challenging conditions: a weightless environment where everything floated, a condensed timeframe, a lab the size of a schoolbus. Every time Roberta wanted to use the microscope to check on samples, for example, she had to reassemble it from storage because of the limited space. She also had to understand, as well as perform, every job on behalf of all the scientists whose experiments were on board. Although she spent some of her time doing the work of a lab technician, tending to plants and recording data, she also had to be trained in many scientific disciplines to troubleshoot when necessary. Fortunately she was not only capable but amazingly versatile.

Other Duties

The IMAX camera was also on board this flight to capture

some of the science for the movie *Destiny in Space*. On top of the astronauts' other duties, NASA expected them to act as photographers as often as possible. As *Discovery* orbited the rotating Earth, 16 times every day, it passed over a slightly different area each time. Before the flight, the members of the crew who were assigned photographic duties had been given a summary of the desired Earth sites, as well as recommended techniques for taking the best pictures.

Roberta was most fascinated watching Earth go by, and the photographer in her was delighted to be able to capture it. She knew that the scientists on the ground needed the invaluable views for forest management and weather forecasting. But taking pictures in space wasn't easy work. Roberta had to restrain herself in the footholds while setting up the camera precisely and in time to catch the required image. It took a lot of energy and concentration. Plus, she wanted to experiment with creative shots, too. Unfortunately, despite the crew's relentless cleaning efforts, in the microgravity environment something was always floating around or sticking to the inside of the windows, preventing a clear view.

Special occasions sometimes interrupted the intense work schedule. Roberta spoke to Prime Minister Brian Mulroney when he called to congratulate her on the great job she was doing on behalf of Canada. The next day, the crew hosted a worldwide press conference. Commander Ron Grabe dedicated the flight to their lost crew member, Sonny

Carter. One of the crew members donned Sonny's favourite baseball cap for the occasion. It helped to remind them all of how precious their time was in space, and on Earth.

The payload scientists' productivity was greatly enhanced by the unprecedented cooperation of the whole crew. Knowing how hard the scientists were working, Ron arranged for the rest of the crew to do as much as possible. They mounted cameras, brought food, and helped out whenever they had the chance. Roberta was even tucked into her sleeping bag one night when she was too tired to fasten her own pillow to the Velcro. On Day Four, because there was power left and everything was running beautifully, the crew was told that the seven-day mission would be extended to eight. Everybody hooted with delight. An extra day gave them even more opportunity for precious data collection in the rare environment of space.

Chapter 9
Living on the Edge

o pilots like Roberta, the shuttle felt more like a submarine than an airplane. But it was a cocoon supporting life in a hostile environment. All they had to do to appreciate it was look out the windows. Minute particles of space debris hitting the vessel could do inordinate damage. The temperature outside the shuttle ranged from a burning hot 150°C to a deep cold of −100°C.

Even though the crowded shuttle had never been meant for long-term space flight, Roberta and the crew had to make do for their week living and working in space. The mid-deck — where the sleeping compartments, galley, and washroom were located — measured only 4 x 4 ¹/₂ metres. It reminded

Roberta of many camping trips, where she had to bunk out in small spaces, eat packaged food, and generally rough it. But there were plenty of differences.

Before they had settled into their respective work routines early in the mission, the crew had a gruesome sight. A puffed-up beach ball floating around turned out to be their packaged sandwiches from launch day. In the excitement of liftoff, they had forgotten to eat lunch. The bacteria had already multiplied in the packaging and produced gas in the plastic bag. They were in space all right!

No Easy Routines

On the shuttle, eating could be a chore and an interruption. Most of the food tended not to be as appetizing as it had been on Earth because astronauts' taste buds changed in space. Apples and other fresh food ran out quickly. Roberta especially missed her beloved skim milk. There was no room for even a tiny fridge in which to store milk in the orbiter's miniature galley kitchen.

When Roberta did find time to eat, she had to rehydrate the dried food by injecting hot or cold water from a needle. Then she kneaded or shook the package until it was moistened and snipped a hole big enough for a spoon to retrieve the contents. Her Girl Guide cookies turned out to be such a hit with her crewmates that she had to hide a few for homesick moments. She thought they tasted even sweeter in space.

One day, as Roberta was eating her supper, she called out a semi-serious warning to her crewmates, "The sauce is loose!" Her shrimp cocktail had lost contact with her spoon. Playing with the food was an amusing contrast to the seriousness of their work, but Roberta also knew what problems food particles could incur. Loose debris floating around in the ship could be dangerous to electrical circuits or experiments, or people. "Sometimes you could be minding your own business, eating something, and suddenly this ball of someone else's food comes and then SPLAT — right on your eyeball."

With no gravity working as a force on her muscles, Roberta noticed they were deteriorating rapidly. Her heart did not have to work as hard in this environment and her legs felt extraordinarily weak. She knew from her research that her bones were becoming brittle, too. Some of the crew were scheduled time on the rowing machine to counter these effects of microgravity and make readjustment to Earth less problematic. Unfortunately for Roberta and Ulf, no time was allotted for their exercise.

Roberta did, however, manage an occasional towel bath, except sometimes keeping clean was more trouble than it was worth. Water did not come down from a shower head but instead floated around. Roberta had to use a wet, rinse-less shampoo, taking care not to stir up soap bubbles, which were hard to get out of the air.

The toilet was also an awkward affair. An astronaut

needed foot and thigh restraints as well as handholds so he or she wouldn't float away. Without gravity, the toilet depended on suction to work. Selecting the correct pump was critical, Roberta had been told repeatedly in training sessions on Earth. The checklist for use and cleanup was long and detailed, and the procedures had to be followed to the letter. For the crew's health and safety, nothing could be permitted to escape into the shuttlecraft's sealed environment. Roberta thought it was ironic that the cleanest place on the shuttle was the bathroom.

If NASA policy hadn't built in compulsory sleep periods into the Payload Crew Activity Plan, Roberta would not have had any time off. More often than not, work spilled into her off time, and she got only two to six hours of sleep per night. When it was her time to rest, looking out the window or fooling around in zero G often felt more important than sleep. Most of the crew had brought along favourite music tapes to lull themselves to sleep. Anne Murray, the Girl Guides, and her own Aunt Erma had all made tapes for Roberta. Bette Midler's "From a Distance" made the perfect background music for her pre-sleep views of the Moon and Earth.

Sleeping on the shuttle was no easy task. The shuttle wall against Roberta's bunk faced the deep cold of space. She bundled up in double sets of long johns and stuffed clothing into cold air jets that were intended to blow carbon dioxide away from her face. Only half joking, she told her crewmates that she preferred to suffocate than freeze to death. The pilot could in fact warm the shuttle by tilting it toward the sun when it wasn't going to affect a delicate experiment in progress. But the payload was considered more important than the crew's comfort — so the astronauts often had to tough it out.

Fun and Games

By the middle of the week, weightlessness had actually become a joy to most of the crew, even the neophytes. Once she was more accustomed to the strange environment, and when she could steal a moment, Roberta joined the space physics games. Giggling like kids, the astronauts squeezed blobs of their drink pouches into the air and grabbed them with open mouths.

One day the crew hosted a most unusual event — the Great Coin Toss — performed during the Super Bowl football game on live TV. Tossing a coin wasn't practical in space of course because it wouldn't fall. Instead, Roberta held the coin while she was flipped by two of her fellow astronauts.

Even while they played, the crew kept their focus on the job. No one had to remind them how little time they had to get everything done. Each *minute* of the flight cost NASA and its partners around $17,000. As a result, there was never enough time to take in the sights, as far as Roberta was concerned. She did, however, interrupt herself in the middle of an experiment one time so that she could see her hometown as they flew over it.

The crew liked to tease the only Canadian aboard. Over the intercom, the pilots announced, "Hey, Roberta, we're going over Canada — *boring*. It's snowbound and inhospitable." Roberta spiritedly disagreed of course. Seeing Canada from this vantage point made a deep impression on her. At a time when constitutional debates were occupying her country, politics seemed irrelevant. From her perspective, there were no unnatural boundaries.

By the end of the jam-packed but productive week, Roberta was looking forward to returning to her favourite place on the planet and sharing all of what she had seen and experienced.

Chapter 10
Coming Down

easuring her fellow astronauts on their last day in space as part of the science experiments, Roberta noted each had grown taller by a couple of inches. Many had been experiencing back pain as a result. Her colleagues on Earth hoped to analyze these findings and extrapolate some benefits for both astronauts and non-astronauts in the future. Very soon, Roberta warned her colleagues, Earth's gravity would literally be dragging them down, both in height and body. They were heading home.

But first, it was time to pack up. Like at the end of a camping trip, a thousand or more individual items had to be stowed away in their proper places. This was no easy task in microgravity. The joke going around was "How many astronauts does it take to close a drawer?" The answer was three. After she stowed the many boxes of plant samples into the Biorack drawer, Roberta pushed against the shuttle's "ceiling" with her arms so her feet would close the lid. Then Steve Oswald and Norm Thagard fastened its clips.

In the process of all the packing, Roberta discovered her glasses. She hadn't realized they were missing because she hadn't needed them since blasting off. Her "space sight" had improved her vision for the entire flight. She was delighted, of course, but as a scientist, wanted to know why. Her hypothesis that shifting fluids within the eye affected the retina or the contour of the cornea would have to wait until Earth to test.

As the Spacelab was regretfully closed down and deactivated, the tunnel from the mid-deck to the lab was closed off for the first time since Day One. The scientific samples Roberta and her team had collected would soon be on their way to the labs on Earth via the world's fastest courier.

Final Tasks

Deciding to catch one more glimpse of Earth before losing her privileged view, Roberta floated up to the flight deck. Earth came into view "incredibly crisp, blue, and vibrant against this deep black of universe." As the pilots prepared for re-entry, the rest of the crew re-assembled the take-down chairs in the mid-deck. They suited up in their re-entry suits, with only one another's help this time, and strapped them-

The crew of STS-42

selves in. Payload and mission specialists alike had to cram into the mid-deck for the next few hours. Only the pilots were on the flight deck, preparing for the last part of their work this mission.

Roberta's work was still not done either. She and Dave

continued to measure each other's blood pressure and heart rates throughout the return voyage. Roberta — this time in her role as doctor — reminded the crew to drink plenty of water before and during the trip down. They also had to ingest salt tablets to retain fluids. Otherwise they'd feel dangerously light-headed when they reached Earth. It was going to be tough enough to re-adapt to gravity. Their blood volume had decreased dramatically since being in space. Pressure garments like Bob Thirsk's experimental antigravity suit helped to stop what they had from rushing to their legs. Used to weighing less than fruit flies, their bodies were already feeling foreign to them as *Discovery* flew closer to Earth — and the forces of gravity. "When we got down through about two-tenths of a G, I could really feel my arms become very heavy," Roberta recalled. What a difference a week in space made!

Return to Earth

Pilot Steve Oswald turned *Discovery*'s tail toward the sun so that its nose pointed at Earth. He slowed the backward and upside-down orbiter by firing the engines just enough for gravity to take effect on the centrifugal force that was holding the shuttle in orbit. They needed gravity to pull *Discovery* toward Earth's atmosphere in a gentle glide. The shuttle still had to leave orbit at exactly the right time and place or it would not land at Edwards Air Force Base in California.

Being strapped in and immobilized again must have

turned Roberta's thoughts to getting home. Her mother would be watching for her in California on the roof over the landing strip, even though NASA policy provided for only spouses and children to be at the landing site. Unmarried, unlike the rest of the crew, Roberta had had to fight hard to get special permission for her mother to greet her.

Crash helmets on, Roberta and the others were bombarded with projectiles they hadn't found or secured in their packing up. The slow banking S-turns helping the shuttle bleed off energy reminded Roberta of downhill skiing. It became harder to talk, and her body felt much heavier. They were almost home, she recognized, but the danger was far from over. Protecting the astronauts from the spectacular pink flames they saw through the window was the shuttle's belly of black ceramic tiles. These would absorb most of the 1620°C heat generated by the friction of striking the atmosphere.

The friction also caused the orbiter to vibrate as it slowed from Mach 25 — 25 times the speed of sound — to only Mach 2. Roberta felt the tugging from her safety harness — the forces of Earth's gravity were really starting to exert themselves. Would they make it down? Radio communication blacked out for a few tense moments. At last they broke through the sound barrier, which buffeted the craft like extreme turbulence. Roberta knew her mother would have heard the separate booms of the nose and the tail as advance notice of what was to come out of the sky. Finally, long seconds after the booms, spectators on the ground would see the shuttle.

Discovery was now visible but still not out of danger. Roberta understood all too well the shuttle had only one chance to make its landing. Without an engine, and at a rapid descent speed of 360 km/h, the pilots had to execute a perfect glide landing. Unlike with ordinary aircraft, there would be no opportunity for another go-round. Ron and Steve had now taken over the full controls from the computer for the final four minutes. Roberta had no doubts about her crewmates' abilities — she just hoped the landing would be soft enough to protect her specimens and film. Following astronaut tradition, the pilots tried to put down precisely on their predecessor's tire marks on the runway. They succeeded. The space shuttle touched down. The astronauts and spectators cheered simultaneously with relief and joy.

Welcome Home

"Roger, *Discovery*, and welcome back ... nice job," came the greeting from the tower, as if it was just another plane coming back from an overseas trip. *Discovery*'s crew had been away more than 193 hours. They had travelled approximately 5,407,000 kilometres, orbiting Earth 129 times.

As much as they wanted to, none of the astronauts could disembark immediately to greet their families. As with any flight, they still had a checklist to follow after they landed. In addition to the usual shutting down of all the equipment, they had to check for toxic gases from unused fuel. Exiting at last, the crew were still wearing their space suits, which now seemed to weigh far more than their 90 pounds. The smells from all the garbage they had brought back with them followed them out the door — hardly an auspicious arrival.

An hour after landing, they were finally able to change into clean, comfortable clothes in the crew transport van. Roberta had a drink without a straw for the first time in eight days. Being back on the ground felt "very, very strange," she told the many curious reporters. She couldn't walk a straight line and had the feeling that she would easily fall over if someone pushed her. It was most unpleasant, she said, but she was glad to be back. "One G [Earth's gravity] is totally underrated. You just have to have one visit to the bathroom to figure that out," she would joke in the endless interviews following her return.

Along with her crewmates, a tired but elated Roberta checked into the clinic for her routine post-flight medical checkup. All the astronauts debriefed only as much as was absolutely necessary before joining their families for hugs, dinner, and a little preview of life back down on Earth. Among other Earthly pleasures, Roberta was looking forward to dipping her feet in the ocean and drinking some cold skim milk.

Epilogue
Life on Earth

For their hero's homecoming celebration on February 19, 1992, two local sisters played a song they had written for her, and Sault Ste. Marie children thronged the city with Canadian flags. Unlike Roberta in the 1950s, these children knew being an astronaut was not a fantasy career anymore. In fact, the Canadian Space Agency had recently announced that a second group of aspiring astronauts would be recruited that summer and trained for the International Space Station.

"It's important to advance the use of space as a new environment for science, to answer the questions we can't answer on Earth." The message Roberta brought to Canadians upon her return was the same one she had spent the past decade championing. Only now she had her own proof — space science was worth the cost and the effort, and could help solve medical problems on Earth. Even before all the debriefing and years of scientific analysis of the IML data still to come, the mission had been hailed a benchmark for international cooperation. Canada was continuing its successful tradition of innovation in aerospace.

But for Roberta, part of history in the making — the

second Canadian astronaut and scientist, the first Canadian woman, and the first neurologist in space — she now had to decide what to do with the rest of her life. Would she remain an astronaut? Would she fly again? Roberta had given eight years of her research career to realizing her dream of flying in space. She had faced incredible scrutiny, roadblocks, and controversy. But she was one of the fortunate to fly.

In the end, she decided she wouldn't be disappointed if she didn't return to space. There were lots of adventures to be had on Earth, too. So, in the summer of 1992, she resigned from the Canadian Astronaut Program to continue her space medical research into the effects of weightlessness on the human body. With her rare first-hand experience, she headed an international team supporting 24 more missions with her Canadian and NASA colleagues.

Since returning to Earth, the self-described "organized tornado" hasn't slowed her pace. She has added 24 more honorary degrees and many other accolades, including the Order of Canada and induction into the Canadian Medical Hall of Fame, to her collection. Concerned by the fragility of the planet she observed from above, she has vowed to protect its health. Roberta has also continued to seriously pursue another of her passions — nature photography. The four books she has authored about her experiences and environmental passions are all accompanied by her photography. Now a well-travelled motivational speaker, she captures attention with her unique perspective: "Very few people can

say I saw my country from space."
　　Roberta had lived her childhood dream.

Appendix 1
Crew of STS-42
January 1992

Commander Ronald (Ron) Grabe
- NASA astronaut — third flight
- Colonel, U.S. Air Force
- Combat fighter pilot, test pilot, and test pilot instructor
- BSc in engineering science

Pilot Stephen (Steve) Oswald
- NASA astronaut — first flight
- Commanding Officer, Naval Space Command Reserve Unit
- Test pilot, flight instructor, flight software verifier
- BSc in aerospace engineering

Flight Engineer William (Bill) Readdy
- NASA astronaut — first flight
- Commander, U.S. Naval Reserve
- Test pilot, test pilot instructor
- BSc in aeronautical engineering

Mission Specialist Norman (Norm) Thagard
- NASA astronaut — fourth flight

- Former Captain, U.S. Marine Corps Reserve
- Naval aviator, researcher, teacher
- BSc, MSc in engineering science, MD

Mission Specialist David (Dave) Hilmers
- NASA astronaut — fourth flight
- Lieutenant Colonel, U.S. Marine Corps
- Pilot
- BSc in mathematics, MSc in electrical engineering

Payload Specialist Ulf Merbold
- European Space Agency astronaut — second flight
- Head of German Aerospace Research Establishment
- Pilot
- PhD physics
- Principal Investigator on IML-1 solid state and low-temperature physics experiment

Payload Specialist Roberta Bondar
- Canadian Space Agency astronaut — first flight
- Pilot, neurologist
- BSc in zoology and agriculture, MSc in experimental pathology, PhD in neurobiology, MD
- Principal Investigator on IML-1 taste experiments, researcher in cerebral blood flow during weightlessness and re-adaptation to Earth

Appendix 2
Timeline

1945   Roberta Bondar born on December 4 to Mildred and Edward Bondar in Sault Ste. Marie, Ontario

1957   Space age begins with *Sputnik*, the world's first artificial satellite, launched by the Soviets. It orbits Earth the same day the Avro Arrow, Canada's new supersonic jet, is unveiled.

1958   National Aeronautics and Space Administration (NASA) is created from the National Advisory Committee for Aeronautics and other U.S. government organizations and almost immediately begins working on options for human space flight

1958   United States launches its first satellite, *Explorer 1*

1959   First flight of Canadian *Black Brant* rocket

1959   First Canadian satellite communications experiment uses the Moon as a reflector

1959   The Avro Arrow project is cancelled, prompting

Canadian aerospace engineers to flock to Project Mercury — NASA's first high-profile effort to learn if humans can survive in space

1960   United States launches *Echo 1*, a giant reflective balloon used in pioneering communications experiments

1961   Yuri Gagarin becomes first person in space, orbiting in *Vostok 1*

1962   *Alouette 1* satellite makes Canada the third country in space

1962   John Glenn is first American to orbit Earth, in Project Mercury's *Friendship 7*

1963   First weather satellite photographs received in Canada

1963   Soviet Valentina Tereshkova becomes first woman in space

1965   NASA's Project Gemini builds upon Mercury's successes and uses spacecraft built for two astronauts

1967   National space agency first recommended for Canada — would not exist until 22 years later

Timeline

1968   Roberta earns a Bachelor's degree from University of Guelph and her private pilot's licence (even before she earns her driver's licence)

1968   NASA's human space flight efforts extend to target the Moon with Project Apollo

1969   Apollo astronauts Neil Armstrong and Buzz Aldrin become first humans to walk on the Moon (Canadian aerospace engineering contributes to the lunar module *Eagle*)

1971   First space station, *Salyut 1*, launched by Soviets

1971   Roberta earns Master's degree from University of Western Ontario, awarded Ontario Graduate Fellowship and National Research Council Scholarships

1972   Final Apollo missions

1972   NASA commits to concept of a reusable space transport system (space shuttle)

1972   David Florida Laboratory (a world-class facility to build and test spacecraft)
opens in Ottawa

1973   Skylab launched by NASA — placed in Earth's orbit to test the concept of a scientific laboratory in space

1974   Roberta earns PhD from University of Toronto, awarded National Research Council (NRC) Postdoctoral Fellowship

1974   NASA awards contract to design and build the world's first Remote Manipulator System for space — Canadarm — to the NRC and Spar Aerospace.

1976   Canada's *Hermes* satellite is launched, becoming the world's most powerful communications satellite

1977   Roberta earns MD from McMaster University

1978   NASA recruits its first female astronauts

1981   Roberta admitted as a Fellow of the Royal College of Physicians and Surgeons of Canada as a specialist in neurology, begins post-graduate neurophthalmology training in Boston and Toronto, and is awarded a Medical Research Council Fellowship

1981   First orbital flight of a NASA space shuttle, *Columbia*

1981   Canadarm is successfully tested during second flight of the space shuttle

1982   Roberta begins professorship at McMaster University, awarded a Career Scientist Award from Ontario Ministry of Health

1982   NASA invites a Canadian on the shuttle at 20th anniversary of Canada-U.S. joint efforts in space, begun with *Alouette*

1983   Sally Ride becomes first American woman in space

1983   NRC's new Canadian Astronaut Program advertises for recruits

1983   Ulf Merbold becomes first non-American payload specialist at NASA to fly

1983   Canada selects six astronauts-to-be: Roberta Bondar, Marc Garneau, Steve MacLean, Bjarni Tryggvason, and Robert Thirsk

1984   Select Six begin astronaut training

1984   Marc Garneau becomes first Canadian to fly

1985   Steve MacLean is chosen for second flight of a Canadian astronaut, set for March 1987

1986   *Challenger* tragedy

1987   MacLean's flight postponed until October 1992

1988   Soviet cosmonauts Titov and Manarov stay in space more than a year — a new record

1988   NASA shuttle flights resume

1989   Canadian Space Agency (CSA) established as independent government agency

1989   Life sciences flight announced by CSA and NASA

1990   Roberta chosen as payload specialist for STS-42 — first International Microgravity Lab mission

1992   International Year of Space

1992   Roberta flies on *Discovery*

1992   Second group of astronauts selected from more than 5000 applicants: Engineer Julie Payette, Dr. Dave Williams, Captain Chris Hadfield, and Robert Stewart, a geophysicist who resigned and was replaced by Captain Mike McKay

1992   Marc Garneau and Chris Hadfield chosen for NASA *mission* specialist training

1992   Roberta resigns from Canadian Astronaut Program to head up an international medical research team at NASA studying the effects of short- and long-term space flight on astronauts from 24 missions over six years

1993   Roberta co-authors a book for children with her sister, Barbara, *On the Shuttle: Eight Days in Space*

1994   Roberta publishes *Touching the Earth*, about her space experiences and environmental concerns

1997   National Gallery of Canada invites Roberta to participate in the exhibition "Science and Photography: Beauty of Another Order"

2000   Roberta exhibits photography and publishes *Passionate Vision: Discovering Canada's National Parks*

2000   Roberta publishes second book of photography, *Canada — Landscape of Dreams*

2003   Roberta installed as Chancellor of Trent University and featured on Canada Post stamp

Appendix 3
Canada's Select Six
— The Other Five

Marc Garneau

Marc was Canada's first astronaut and its most travelled, logging 677 hours in space. His second flight was Mission STS-77 on *Discovery* in May 1996 and his third was on *Endeavour* to the International Space Station in 2000. Holding a doctorate in electrical engineering, he had been seconded to the astronaut program from the Canadian navy, where he served as commander and expert in naval communications and electronic warfare equipment and systems. He retired from the navy and as an active astronaut to become the president of the Canadian Space Agency in 2001.

Steve MacLean

Youngest of the original six astronauts selected, "the kid" holds a PhD in physics, with a specialty in laser physics and space robotics. He served as program manager for Advanced Space Vision System, a computer-based camera system designed to provide guidance data that enhances the control of Canadarm.

Steve followed Roberta into space on *Columbia* as a payload specialist for mission STS-52. Afterward, he became the chief science advisor for the International Space Station (ISS) and, later, director general of the Canadian Astronaut Program. Also trained as a mission specialist, he was assigned to his second flight to visit the ISS before the shuttle program was again cancelled due to the loss of *Columbia* in February 2003.

Ken Money

As a former Olympic high jumper and a parachutist, Ken was accustomed to flying high. But he was never able to parlay his PhD in physiology and experience flying fighter aircraft, bush planes, and helicopters into a space shuttle flight. After backing up Roberta on her 1992 mission, Ken retired at the age of 57. He returned to the Defence and Civil Institute of Environmental Medicine in Toronto as a senior scientist to research, write academic papers, and lecture at universities. He also continued to consult for NASA.

Robert Thirsk

In addition to his science and engineering degrees, Bob has a medical degree and an MBA. As a biomedical engineering researcher, he investigated the effects of weightlessness on the body and designed an experimental anti-gravity suit, which Roberta's flight helped test.

Bob's first assignment was as backup to Marc Garneau. He later led national space-education classroom projects, Tomatosphere and Canolab, which grew plants from space-flown seeds. He trained as a mission specialist and served as a CAPCOM (Capsule Communicator), relaying communications between flight controllers at Mission Control and the International Space Station crew during space flights at Johnson Space Center.

Bjarni Tryggvason
Bjarni's wait for a flight was five years longer than Roberta's. He was 51 by the time he followed Marc, Roberta, Steve, Chris Hadfield, and Bob into space. While waiting his turn, the airline-rated pilot and engineer conducted flight experiments. In 1997, Bjarni finally blasted off on board the same space shuttle as Roberta, *Discovery*. STS-85 was an 11-day mission to study changes in Earth's atmosphere and prepare for the International Space Station (ISS). NASA later invited Bjarni to take part in mission specialist training, as part of the first group of astronauts to be trained as both mission specialists for the space shuttle and as potential crew members for the ISS.

Bibliography

Bondar, Barbara, and Bondar, Roberta. *On the Shuttle: Eight Days in Space.* Toronto: Greey de Pencier Books, 1993.

Bondar, Roberta. *Touching the Earth.* Toronto: Key Porter Books, 1994.

Dotto, Lydia. *The Astronauts.* Toronto: Stoddart, 1993.

Dotto, Lydia. *Canada in Space.* Toronto: Irwin, 1987.

Reichhardt, Tony. *Space Shuttle: The First 20 Years — The Astronauts' Experiences in Their Own Words.* Washington: DK Publishing, 2002.

Acknowledgments

Roberta Bondar is a popular speaker and teacher who has generously shared her experiences as an astronaut and scientist with the Earth-bound through her talks, interviews, awe-inspiring photography, and thought-provoking books. Both Dr. Bondar and Christine Yankou, editor and managing director of Roberta Bondar Astronaut Enterprise, found time in their busy schedules to review the facts from this slice of Roberta's life. Raymonde Champagne, from the Canadian Space Agency's library, was most encouraging and provided invaluable resources. Linda Burtch, caretaker of the papers that Dr. Bondar donated to the Sault Ste. Marie Library (the official home of the Roberta Bondar archives), assisted in a long-distance way. Lydia Dotto's books are invaluable and delightful accounts of Canada's involvement in space that springboarded this one. My appreciation goes to them all, to Altitude (Kara, Jill, and Lori), and to Frances and Lisa for facilitating the telling of this amazing story.

For the research and quotations in this book, I am indebted to Dr. Bondar's and Ms. Dotto's books as well as to interviews by journalists at the time: David Macfarlane (*Saturday Night*); Robert Miller, Hilary Mackenzie, and June Rogers (*Maclean's*); Sally Armstrong (*Canadian Living*);

Acknowledgments

Charlotte Gray and John Colapinto (*Chatelaine*); Paula Todd and Dianne Rinehart (*Homemaker's*); and Bill Knapp (*Aviation and Aerospace*), as well as to the Canadian Space Agency, which recorded mission briefings, press conferences, and pre-flight and post-flight interviews.

About the Author

A long-time stargazer and armchair astronaut herself, Joan Dixon welcomed this chance to tell the story of one of Canada's very own space pioneers. Stories of Canadians who have done incredible things have always been inspiration for her research and writing projects. Her last book for the Amazing Stories series was *Trailblazing Sports Heroes: Exceptional Personalities and Outstanding Achievements in Canadian Sport.*

Photo Credits

All photographs are provided courtesy of Dr. Roberta Bondar. Additional cedits are as follows. Cover: NASA; NASA: page 62, 78, 89, 103.

OTHER AMAZING STORIES

ISBN	Title	Author
1-55153-943-8	Black Donnellys	Nate Hendley
1-55153-947-0	Canada's Rumrunners	Art Montague
1-55153-966-7	Canadian Spies	Tom Douglas
1-55153-795-8	D-Day	Tom Douglas
1-55153-982-9	Dinosaur Hunters	Lisa Murphy-Lamb
1-55153-970-5	Early Voyageurs	Marie Savage
1-55153-968-3	Edwin Alonzo Boyd	Nate Hendley
1-55153-996-9	Emily Carr	Cat Klerks
1-55153-973-X	Great Canadian Love Stories	Cheryl MacDonald
1-55153-946-2	Great Dog Stories	Roxanne Snopek
1-55153-942-X	The Halifax Explosion	Joyce Glasner
1-55153-958-6	Hudson's Bay Company Adventures	Elle Andra-Warner
1-55153-969-1	Klondike Joe Boyle	Stan Sauerwein
1-55153-980-2	Legendary Show Jumpers	Debbie G-Arsenault
1-55153-775-3	Lucy Maud Montgomery	Stan Sauerwein
1-55153-964-0	Marilyn Bell	Patrick Tivy
1-55153-953-5	Moe Norman	Stan Sauerwein
1-55153-962-4	Niagara Daredevils	Cheryl MacDonald
1-55153-945-4	Pierre Elliott Trudeau	Stan Sauerwein
1-55153-991-8	Rebel Women	Linda Kupecek
1-55153-956-X	Robert Service	Elle Andra-Warner
1-55153-952-7	Strange Events	Johanna Bertin
1-55153-954-3	Snowmobile Adventures	Linda Aksomitis
1-55153-950-0	Tom Thomson	Jim Poling Sr.
1-55153-976-4	Trailblazing Sports Heroes	Joan Dixon
1-55153-977-2	Unsung Heroes of the RCAF	Cynthia J. Faryon
1-55153-959-4	A War Bride's Story	Cynthia Faryon
1-55153-948-9	The War of 1812 Against the States	Jennifer Crump

These titles are available wherever you buy books. If you have trouble finding the book you want, call the Altitude order desk at 1-800-957-6888, e-mail your request to: orderdesk@altitudepublishing.com or visit our Web site at www.amazingstories.ca

New AMAZING STORIES titles are published every month.